Who Am I and Where Is Home?

An American Woman in 1931 Palestine

Who Am I and Where Is Home?
An American Woman in 1931 Palestine

by
Andrea Jackson

St. Louis, Missouri

ISBN: 978-0-692-87238-3
Library of Congress Control Number: 2017906094

Cover design and interior by Cathy Wood Book Design

Andrea Jackson
www.AndreaJackson.net

To my husband, Bob Jackson,
and our children and grandchildren

The Dream Keeper

Bring me all of your dreams,
You dreamer.
Bring me all of your heart melodies
That I may wrap them in a blue cloud-cloth
Away from the too-rough fingers of the world.

—Langston Hughes

CONTENTS

Chapter 1   The farthest adventure yet   **1**

Chapter 2   I must fill my eyes with innocence   **9**

Chapter 3   There is no rebellion among the Buffalonians   **11**
*(Letters from Ellis Polonsky to Celia Antopolsky,
September 19, 1930 to October 16, 1930)*

Chapter 4   I can't enjoy my spaghetti without you   **21**
*(Correspondence between Harry Neiman and
Celia Antopolsky, September 18, 1930 to
October 19, 1930)*

Chapter 5   Bullets in her bra   **27**

Chapter 6   Dear friend of a sudden meeting   **35**
*(Correspondence between Harry Neiman and
Celia Antopolsky, February 6, 1930 and November 1
to November 5, 1930)*

Chapter 7   We know how to do this   **41**

Chapter 8   The most stirring speech ever made   **47**
*(Letters from Ellis Polonsky to Celia Antopolsky,
October 21, 1930 to November 18, 1930)*

Chapter 9   If an Arab approaches you menacingly   **59**
(Lillian Shapiro's impressions of life in Jerusalem)

Chapter 10   They knew they couldn't stop us   **67**

Chapter 11   Station IKE   **71**
*(Correspondence between Celia Antopolsky and
her family, November 14, 1930 to February 12, 1931)*

Chapter 12   An ivory cigarette holder   **83**

Chapter 13   "To see the World as Beauty"   87
              (Letters from Ellis Polonsky to Celia Antopolsky,
              November 21, 1930 to November 28, 1930)

Chapter 14   Dear Boy   91
              (Correspondence between Harry Neiman
              and Celia Antopolsky, December ___ 1930
              to February 25, 1931)

Chapter 15   Shout through the streets of Zion   105
              (Letters from Ellis Polonsky to Celia Antopolsky,
              December 17, 1930 to February 26, 1931)

Chapter 16   Ellis, sex, and Nietzsche   123
              (Excerpts from Celia Antopolsky's journal,
              November 28, 1928 to May 25, 1929)

Chapter 17   Are you too moulding dream hills?   125
              (Letters from Ellis Polonsky to Celia Antopolsky,
              January 29, 1931 to April, 1931)

Chapter 18   Dearest far-away family   131
              (Correspondence between Celia Antopolsky and
              her family, February 12, 1931 to April 15, 1931)

Chapter 19   Smug complacency and stupid egotism   139
              (Letters between Celia Antopolsky and
              Harry Neiman, March 12, 1931 to June 1, 1931)

Chapter 20   Please, Celia—destroy this letter   145
              (Correspondence between Lillian Shapiro and
              Celia Antopolsky, March 20, 1931 to April 27, 1931)

Chapter 21   I am sincere in my emotions   157
              (Letters from Ellis Polonsky to Celia Antopolsky,
              April 6, 1931 to July, 1931)

Chapter 22   You see, we really want you to come home   **169**
              (Correspondence between Celia Antopolsky and
              her family, April 17, 1931 to September 24, 1931)

Chapter 23   "Did she fall in love with someone there?"   **177**
              (Correspondence among Celia Antopolsky,
              Lillian Shapiro and Joey Marks, May 4, 1931
              to August 26, 1931)

Chapter 24   Languidly, I think of going back   **191**
              (Correspondence between Harry Neiman and
              Celia Antopolsky, June 23, 1931 to
              November 16, 1931)

Chapter 25   Cable her to meet the boat   **205**
              (Correspondence between Lillian Shapiro
              and Celia Antopolsky, August 27, 1931 to
              December 5, 1931)

Chapter 26   So full a year as we have had   **219**
              (Letter and telegram from Ellis Polonsky to
              Celia Antopolsky, December 1 and 2, 1931)

Chapter 27   This is how people go out of your life   **221**
              (Letters from Ruth Light, a friend in Jerusalem,
              to Celia Antopolsky, December 3, 1931 and
              January 31, 1932)

Chapter 28   The American girl from Jerusalem   **225**

Chapter 29   Fourteen days on that boat   **229**

Chapter 30   Afterword   **233**

*Above: Lillian, Celia
and Ellis, Washington
Square, New York
City, c.1927*

*Right: Lillian and
Celia on graduation
day from New York
University*

Commencement: June 6, 1928

Gilbert and Sullivan

Chapter 1

The farthest adventure yet

Celia Antopolsky emerged from the subway into brilliant sunlight. The docks were crowded with tall ships and steamboats, each in its own slip. Clouds of steam floated toward the open sky.

She was dressed for travel in a brown twill suit, opaque stockings, and sturdy shoes. She wore no hat, letting her curly blond-brown hair float freely. The hair was unmanageable, and rather than try to tamp it down, she had chosen to turn it into a trademark. In her passport photo, it rises above her head like a flame, as if her head were on fire. She would never be pretty like her sisters, Betty and Minna, but never mind. She would be distinctive. She would get by on charm.

With her, clustering around her, blocking her way almost, was the family. Celia was twenty-four years old and a college graduate, the first in her family; but family is forever, and they had all come to see her off—her mother, brother Irving, sister Minna, married sister Betty with her little girl—all but Papa, who never took time off from work except for the Jewish holidays and *Shabbat* [the Sabbath].

It was September 18, 1930. A boy hawked papers, "German political situation improved"—but who had time, money, or interest to read about Europe? The man selling Red Hot Frankfurters and Ice Cold Lemonade wasn't getting many takers, either. In these hard times people brought their own lunches. The air was dense with the smells of pastrami and heavy spices.

The autumn air was chilly. Two-year-old Joanie, Celia's niece, started to cry as a gust of wind blew into her face. Her mother, Celia's older sister Betty, picked Joanie up and tried to shield her while dodging the people who were hurrying in all directions.

Lillian Shapiro was already at the dock, smiling at them. Petite, brown-eyed, with smooth dark hair gathered into a bun at the back of her neck: If Celia was a flame, Lillian was a small brown bird. At the sight of her, Celia's anxiety, after a sleepless night and a morning filled with last-minute packing and hurried messages from family and neighbors, evaporated. Lillian was Celia's alter ego, her close friend since girlhood and her companion on adventures—the instigator, really. They had hitch-hiked from Brooklyn up to Montreal, down the Eastern seaboard, across the United States and back. Celia and Lillian had had homemade leather patches on their backpacks: *New York to California, Round the World!* People laughed to see them, called them "delightful hoboes."

Celia's weatherbeaten backpack was filled with miscellany that hadn't made it into her traveling trunk. She hoisted it onto her shoulder and joined Lillian, followed by the little cluster of Antopolskys. Celia's brother Irving held Mama's arm. Betty adjusted Joanie's position on her hip. Minna, the youngest sibling at eighteen, trailed behind, amusing herself by watching the swarm of men and boys working on the docks or just hanging around.

Celia and Lillian were boarding the French cargo ship *Alesia* for a passage from New York to Palestine, their farthest adventure yet. In its 28-day journey across the Atlantic the ship would stop at exotic cities to load and unload cargo and passengers, and Celia and Lillian would have chances to go sightseeing.

Palestine, the "Promised Land" of the Old Testament, had been controlled by the Ottoman Empire for centuries. The Empire had been finally broken up in the World War, which ended in 1918, and now the loosely defined area known as Palestine was controlled by the British, who were supposedly holding it for the Jews under instructions from the League of Nations, but whose intentions were doubtful. Arabs who had lived there for centuries, though never technically owners, claimed rights to the land; meanwhile, groups of Jews had been establishing colonies in Palestine for decades, some having purchased land from the legal owners, and others simply relying on the Biblical claim of the Jews. France claimed an interest because of some wartime arrangements with Britain. No one knew how it might turn out.

Celia had no money for such a trip. But Lillian's father, a third-generation immigrant with a share in his family's sign-painting business, had set aside money every month as a sort of dowry for Lillian, and he drew on it, at Lillian's request, to pay for the girls' trip to Palestine. He gave them $1,000 to share, an astonishing sum.

"You can pay me back," Lillian said to Celia, "when you marry a rich man," an event both of them thought was as likely as not, considering the triumphs Celia had had in her life so far: The winner, in high school, of several city-wide essay contests, she had been the first woman to be elected vice president of her college class. Already, she had been a "stringer" for a newspaper, and her poetry and stories had been published in literary magazines.

They had splurged and bought first-class tickets for the trip to Palestine, $195 each, so they could share a cabin instead of sleeping in a dormitory. Each ticket covered accommodations aboard ship and meals. The money for Celia's return fare was safe in the Bank of the United States, a neighborhood bank that catered mostly to immigrant Jews like her parents.

Everyone was shouting greetings, farewell messages, cautions, expressed in a din of languages: English, Hebrew, Yiddish, and other languages Celia didn't recognize. It seemed that she and Lillian were at the center of the gesturing, jabbering, excited crowd, as if all the others had been assembled only for them, to see them off on their adventure. It would

3

have been perfect, if only Ellis had been there.

And there he was, a head taller than most of the passengers and their friends and relatives. Unlike many of them, he had been born in America and benefited from an American diet. Tall and lean, hunched and blond, with his lips in a thin smile, he seemed almost unaware of the excitement surrounding him. Celia spotted him, and, next to him, his friend Joey Marks, an Englishman who had come to America to visit relatives, met Lillian Shapiro, and decided to stay. Celia turned away, feigning unconcern, as the two men pushed through the crowd.

The young man at the gangplank announced: "Passengers may board now. Show your tickets, please. Family and friends, if you want to come aboard, sign in here and make sure you're out by 2:30. We'll ring the bell at quarter past two."

Mama was looking for someplace to sit down. Her legs weren't so good these days, and her attacks of asthma were becoming more frequent. "I'll stay with her," Betty said, with a martyred sigh.

Joey took Lillian's hand and pulled her away until they were hidden from the others by a little knot of travelers and well-wishers. He took both her hands in his and said urgently, "You must come back. You must come back soon."

Lillian colored and laughed. "But why wouldn't I come back?"

"Come back to me."

"Two or three months, that's all. I promise."

Ellis stood by Celia's side, his silent presence warming her. Impulsively, she said, "I wish you were coming with us."

"So do I."

"Remember to write," she said.

"I'll write you a letter today." He looked down at her. "Would you like that?"

"And tomorrow."

"My comerado will receive so many letters from me that she will tire of them. She will write and say, *Dayenu*, my comerado! Enough with the letters!"

"No, I won't."

"Ah, you say that now."

With the *Alesia* about to pull out of the harbor, all the well-wishers had been shooed off the ship. The girls stood at the rail and waved to the crowd.

Mama was already crying. In her experience, to send a person off on a boat was never to see them again.

She and Papa had been among the thousands of immigrants to America in the early years of the twentieth century. Like many other Jews, they had fled Central Europe, understanding that their lives were in constant danger from Christian massacres, known as "pogroms."

"Hush, Ma," said Irving. "You're embarrassing us."

"Who cares embarrassing," said Mama. She looked up at the ship. "Look." She gestured toward Celia.

Celia laughed at them and mouthed something.

"I don't know what she's saying," Mama complained.

"She says, 'I'll see you soon,'" said Betty.

"No, she doesn't. She says, 'Stay out of my room,'" said Irving, thinking that was what he would have said in her place.

"No, she says, 'Minna can have my green sweater,'" said Minna.

"She does not," said Betty.

Having watched the ship sail away, the girls waving at the rail, Ellis and Joey drifted with the crowd toward the street.

"Well, then," Joey said. "Off to pound the pavements. Best find a job before they ship me back across the pond."

"Lucky you."

"What do you mean?" asked Joey.

"All you have to do is find a job. You will. You're smart, and with that classy accent, you sound like a radio announcer."

Joey grinned. "Aww, you poor bastard. Just what do you have to worry about?"

Suddenly, spontaneously, Ellis burst out, "God, I wish I were going with them."

"Now, now. She'll be back in three months or so, won't she?"

"I don't mean that. I have bigger worries," Ellis said. "Transcendent worries, worries that you with your money-grubbing little brain could not begin to imagine, let alone comprehend."

"Let me guess. You have a thesis to write for school and you haven't started your research."

"That plus the state of the world. Don't you read? The Nazis are taking over Germany. They're going to drive us out of Europe."

"Us?"

"The Jews, as you know perfectly well. It's not funny."

"And yet you still have a thesis to do, and I still don't have a job. See you later?"

"I don't know. Maybe. Depends," Ellis said.

"Depends?" Joey teased. "I foresee a visit to the beauteous Lee Kaplan."

"I just wish I were doing something useful this winter," Ellis said, gazing toward the ocean. Even now, in Palestine, others were crafting the institutions, shaping the structure of government and society. By the time he might manage to get there, it could be too late.

Under the clouds, the wind, and the setting sun, the ocean, no longer blue and smiling, turned shifting, uncertain colors. Celia wrapped the jacket of her travel suit closely around her.

Lillian had gone below, leaving Celia alone at the rail. Without an audience, Celia's brave front disappeared. Her nighttime anxiety returned, this time with thoughts of the little *Alesia*, storm-tossed, struggling, and finally sinking hopelessly into the sea.

Ellis Polonsky to Celia, September 18, 1930, 6:00 p.m.

Miss Celia Antopolsky
Aboard S. S. Alesia Rm 233
c/o Fabre Line
Jaffa
Palestine

Fabre Line note!
If undelivered please forward to Poste Restante, Tel Aviv, Palestine

Shalom my comerado—

Welcome home. It is our land. Take off your pack and smile. You and your people have wandered sufficiently. Rest here in security.

Step forward with assurance, it is your land I tell you. Your forefathers have nurtured it, tended it and built it. Others have neglected and destroyed. Once again, your sisters and brothers have cleaned it and rebuilt it.

It matters not what others say. The land is ours and you are home.

My comerado—I rejoice with you and greet you.

Ellis

Joey and Ellis

Chapter 2

I must fill my eyes with innocence

The year is 1952. I am ten years old, still small enough to sit in the middle of the front seat between my parents, over the hump of the driveshaft. My father drives, as always.

My mother says to me, "Don't you think Dad looks handsome today?"

I turn to look at his profile. It is the same as usual.

"Yes," I say, finally.

My father keeps his eyes on the road but smiles his familiar closed-mouthed smile, a smile of pleasure and pain commingled, seeming to register that he is pleased with the compliment but knows it falls short in some way and, besides, that it doesn't really matter in the scheme of things. It is the smile he wears in the old photographs of my parents at one of the family functions they rarely attended, or on the boat when they took a cruise, once, to Europe. My mother, beaming open-mouthed into the camera, projecting her whole personality toward the documentation that was being generated, and my father with his pained smile seeming to bear on his shoulders the awareness of work waiting undone, of superficial friends being encouraged for no reason, of bills unpaid and accruing even at that moment.

I know, even then, that my mother isn't really asking for my opinion. She is trying to say something nice to my father, just a nonspecific nice thing. But for some reason she can't, or won't, speak to him directly.

My mother kept every letter she received during her long life, along with some she had written and mailed and somehow gotten back from the recipients, and others she had begun to write and abandoned unfinished.

After her death, I found them stashed helter-skelter in desk drawers, dresser drawers, mislabeled file folders; mixed with bank statements; and at the back of the linen closet behind the folded white curtain, dingy with age, that had been an improvised veil at my parents' slapdash wedding ceremony.

Armed with the letters, I began to tackle the mystery that pervaded the life of our family. What had happened, back in the past, to make him so cautious with her, to make her so chary of showing affection?

The story, I learned, began before their marriage, back when she was Celia Antopolsky, the middle Antopolsky daughter, the one who did so well in school.

Among her papers, I find this poem, which she wrote before she was married:

Diffidence

You stammer, rudely inarticulate,
    And choke upon the words of golden flame,
You murmur banal talk and think to hide
    The glow about your accent of my name.

And I must fill my eyes with innocence,
    Must laugh away the daggers subtly veiled,
Lest you may some day look too deep,
    And seeing, dare to win where I have failed.

Chapter 3

There is no rebellion among the Buffalonians
(Letters from Ellis Polonsky to Celia Antopolsky,
September 19, 1930 to October 16, 1930)

Ellis to Celia, September 19, 1930, 7:30 p.m.

Miss Celia Antopolsky
Aboard S. S. Alesia Rm 233
c/o Fabre Line
Jaffa
Palestine

Fabre Line Note!
If undelivered forward to Poste Restante, Tel Aviv, Palestine

Marca [*a nickname suggesting that Celia is a female Marco Polo, i.e., a traveler*]—
I would find a way to come to you on the breast of a wave, or through
the song of a wild sea bird. At a time when you miss me most I would steal
through your porthole—hide under your bed—surprise you at your table
—or meet you as you turn a corner. But a sea's a sea and I've lost my seven
league boots—the kind that are waterproof.
When word came from you I knew it was Providence that was so kind
to me. And when you are lonely and I'm not round, you shan't be lonely,
for Walt [Whitman] is with you. Others will be lonely and inconsolably so,
but they have not found the maternal comforter Walt. You can find me in

him and I can find you in him—our Walt.

City life slides into a rather pathetic groove—rebellion or no. Even in my little way I shall have to be getting up and going, I shall have to find more to do and more to do it with to fill a gap that I knew was being made by my Comerado's going to sea.

I have no work at present and plan little or no schooling but I never suffered because [of] the lack of either.

I have impatiently awaited a copy of Poet and Critic and it has not come. On my infantile side I have written a story which I like very much. It is developed in the present Russian setting and involves the anti-religious campaign and a crippled little songbird—a boy of twelve. You shall have an early copy.

Yours for Zion,

Ellis

One of five poems by Celia Antopolsky, published, along with a story, in the journal *The Poet and the Critic*, September, 1930, under the pen name Sevia Antopolska:

Song

This is the song of my coming to you,
    Unfasten my crown,
    Press down my wings,
Take from my shoulders the garland I wear,
Set only love for a flower in my hair.

Fashion the song of my coming to you,
    Its warm joy alone
    Covering shall be,
If I am left naked upon the hill,
If your eyes grow sullen, if your lips are still

Ellis to Celia, dated Rosh Hashanah [the Jewish New Year, which began at sunset on September 22]. This letter was postmarked September 27, 1930 from Fox Street Station, New York City.

Marca,

May my comerado be inscribed for a beautiful and happy year. The first day of the year has added considerably to your fame. T*he Poet and Critic* has arrived and I am certain it can thrill you no more than it has me. It was delivered in the midst of a delicious holiday meal, which I passed up immediately because of my state of excitement.

In the last hour, I have read and reread your story and there are so many beautiful bits of description that I'm sure could not have been equaled by anyone. And your (I almost feel like saying "our poems") poems have the delicacy and wistfulness of Teasdale, the color of Fletcher and the feeling of Marca. They imply great inspiration—who or what was the inspiration!

Marca it is all so beautiful that I feel a lump in my throat, and that Emily Dickinson said was the test of a great poem. I think you are beginning to threaten Frost's position in my poetry evaluation.

Well, now that you're great—may I be so humble as to relate my meager existence. Tired and bored with nothing to do here, I am departing these parts and going for a week visit and trip to Buffalo from where I expect to be taken touring Canada and thereabouts.

Weather here is warm and things are dull. Have no job as yet, so I continue to vacation. The very ennui of existence makes writing without repetition impossible—so au revoir,

Your severest critic who still remains,

Your comerado,

Ellis

MARRIAGE CERTIFICATE

I, _Chaim Davidovich_, a _rabbi_ residing at _313 Pratt_ in the city of _Buffalo_ in county of _Erie_ and state of New York, do hereby certify that I did on the _27_ day of _September_ in the year A.D. 19_30_, at Buffalo, in the county of Erie and state of New York, solemnize the rites of matrimony between _Ellis Polonsky_ . . . and _Elizabeth Kaplan_ . . . . Witness my hand at Buffalo in the county of Erie this _27_ day of _September_ A.D. 19_30_.

From Ellis's point of view, Lee Kaplan was a far more sensible choice as a spouse than Celia would have been. Lee was a good sport who would accept a lot of self-centered behavior from Ellis. Also, unlike Celia, she knew how to cook and generally maintain a household.

Nevertheless, he went to great lengths to conceal from Celia the fact that he had married Lee on September 27, 1930, just a few days after Celia's ship had left for Palestine. For starters, he arranged for his Rosh Hashanah letter to be mailed in New York City on the very day of his wedding in Buffalo. On October 7 and 8 he wrote her two long and sprightly letters emphasizing the tedium of his trip to Buffalo and implying that he went there alone.

Ellis to Celia, October 7, 1930

Miss Celia Antopolsky
Poste Restante
Tel Aviv
Palestine

Marca, comerado—

Gee but it's good to sit down again and talk to you across the table. You have now regained complete control of your land legs and I of my ability to just sit still and think and talk to you.

You have gone thousands of miles and seen quiet and simple beauty, I have gone hundreds and heard noisy and advertised effects. You are in the enviable position, I in the envying position.

I have been to Buffalo, Niagara and Canada—a trip that has been built, advertised and used for honeymoons. In fact I have been accused of even that since I returned from Niagara.

The trip to and from Buffalo by bus consists of eighteen hours of riding that was remarkably uneventful and tiring. It was taken in the bleak coldness that induces despair and encourages one, snail-like, to crawl into one's shell . . .

. . . Buffalo, New York's second largest city, is large, spacious, but dull. Its people think slowly and in small areas. There is no rebellion among the Buffalonians, the only rebellion lies with those exiles from New York who are faced by circumstance to live there. My stay in Buffalo was cut short because I could not find enough diversion in the vicinity to keep me from being bored. Life there consists of social calls after social calls with bridge thrown in now and then to fill a gap.

—To be continued—
Your comerado, Ellis

Ellis to Celia, October 8, 1930

Miss Celia Antopolsky
Poste Restante
Tel Aviv
Palestine

Marca chavera [friend]—

Before I continue to the Falls, let me grasp your hand firmly and ask how you are. Are you lonely? Are you at home? Have you found a greater beauty in Palestine than you have found in the dazzling white Algiers or the

Blue Azores? Has Palestine's earnestness and simplicity touched you more?

Since my last letter nothing unusual has happened. I am taking just one course at N.Y.U. for no earthly reason. I am doing testing work voluntarily for the Brooklyn Continuation School, which has an enrollment of 10,000 boys. I have (like Joey Marks) a prospect of a psychologist position in Long Beach L.I. I have a thesis to complete and bread to be earned.

The ride from Buffalo to the Falls covers such level and monotonous land that one finds oneself bored and yawny. Only at rare occasions one sees an inhabitant or a cultivated field . . . .

The falls were disappointing, not for what it was but for what man has made it. The advertising and the utilizing have taken the heart out of it. Picture if it had been left in its primeval surroundings and no one knew of its existence, and one climbed high hills in vigorous and earnest search for beauty and suddenly the falls come into view. Clinging tightly one watched undirected the crash of these waters and discovered that rainbow and looked down and into a bridgeless and boatless gorge. Now I question whether the falls and even the rainbow are natural.

Marca—I salute you—Ellis

Ellis to Celia, October 13, 1930 (date of Celia and Lillian's arrival in Palestine)

Comerado of far away places—

It is a miracle to me that a letter that bears the stamp of a strange land that lies thousands of miles away from me can draw me so close to you.

How good it was to hear that you are being caught in the dazzling life of these different lands and that you like it. How glad I am to know that my comerado is extending her conquests to strange sounding lands and is finding the beauty there. For the soul of my comerado is like a most delicate sponge that can absorb beauty and contain it, while the souls of others are just the trailing fingers in the water, that feel it but dry quickly.

And you my Queen of Israel—see to it that your husband builds a sturdy temple, convince him of the value of modern improvements, electric lights, steam heat, umbrella racks, etc. And above all make him a benevolent and tolerant king. And if he's looking for a Minister of Education, speak to him of me, tell him of my qualifications and perhaps I can become a courtier and play with death by wooing the Queen. After all did not his forefather steal Bath Sheba from Uriah the Hittite.

Things are crawling along here at not too great a pace. Personally I am not in the proverbial pink suffering these last few days from a very painful sore throat. It hasn't affected my singing voice, fortunately.

Psychological positions are very few because they are still considered a luxury and all organizations are running on minimum budgets due to the most miserable economic conditions prevailing. Young Judaea [an organization intended to interest young people into moving to Palestine; Ellis worked there, sometimes for pay and sometimes as a volunteer] has no money and hence no activity.

My only means of support comes from Sunday School and an occasional story but I don't care—I'll wait until my ship comes in.

The last I saw of Marks, he was busy on an advertising venture which involved thousands while in his jacket he had a mere 20¢. But there's no telling, he might get there.

Edna Sue, Josh and I were up to visit Frankie and Wally was strangely away. I have a luncheon appointment with Wally and I shall try to see if there exist any domestic difficulties.

How meagre I feel this letter must be, but Marca, I do not travel from port to port as you do. I am rooted to a spot you know well.

Put your pack on Marca, face the east and climb the Mount of Olives. It's good to perspire—in one's own land.

Shalom,
Your comerado,
Ellis

Ellis to Celia, October 16, 1930

Marca—

It is the business of a comerado to come when one needs a comerado most, to come even over fathomless seas—and above all to know when to come.

I shall never forget how happy I was to know that my little gift of the book "Fireflies" came when you wanted and needed it—and how I felt that I must have been a comerado—how happy to have you and you to have me when we needed each other. I rejoiced in the fact that I could tell in a flash when you needed my arms about you and when you wanted me to mother you—and that's a comerado. I knew when you wanted me in quiet distance placed—and that's a comerado.

So when I was in bed with a miserable case of tonsillitis and night passed so painfully slowly and I faced dawn with no relief and thoughts of you kept me looking East, a letter from Azores—a beautiful letter came and I wondered how you knew I wanted you then and beauty—but that's a comerado.

Whether it was this morning's bright letter or the "love and gladness" you sent, I do not know—but I am better and the sun is shining. What lies outside I do not think of because thoughts can only lead to disappointments. So I run away from all of this and flee to the arms of my comerado and side by side we stare open mouthed at all about us.

I celebrated this week because on Tuesday my comerado came home to Palestine and I am happy and proud. "Say what you want," she said one day, "you'll never make me a Zionist." "In search of beauty and a cause," she wrote on the back of envelopes, to me, from her trip west. And then I hoped the beauty and the cause she would find in the east. And I know she will.

For when my comerado loves, she loves with a fiery zeal—and when she sees beauty she cannot help but be part of it and live it. That's a comerado.

What lies outside I do not think of because thoughts can only lead to disappointments. So I run away from all of this and flee to the arms of my comerado. Of myself, let me say nothing, there is nothing to say.

I cannot write more this time, I feel strongly our tie of comeraderie.

Marca, I salute you
Ellis

From Walt Whitman, *Song of the Open Road*:

> Camerado, I give you my hand!
> I give you my love more precious than money,
> I give you myself before preaching or law;
> Will you give me yourself? will you come travel with me?
> Shall we stick by each other as long as we live?

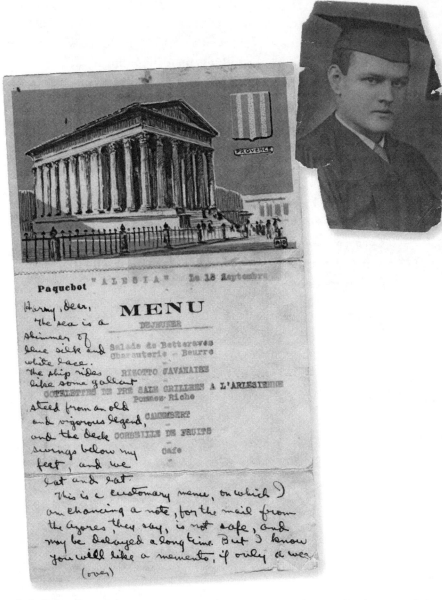

Paquebot "ALESIA" le 18 Septembre

MENU
DEJEUNER

Harry, dear,
The sea is a shimmer of blue silk and white lace.
The ship rides like some gallant steed from an old and vigorous legend, and the deck swings below my feet, and we eat and eat.
This is a customary menu, on which I am chancing a note, for the mail from the Azores, they say, is not safe, and may be delayed a long time. But I know you will like a memento, if only a wee—
(over)

Left: Letter from Celia to Harry. Top right: Harry on graduation day from St. John's College School of Law, which was then the only New York law school that accepted Jewish students.

Chapter 4

I can't enjoy my spaghetti without you

(Correspondence between Harry Neiman and Celia Antopolsky,
September 18, 1930 to October 19, 1930)

Harry to Celia, September 18, 1930

HARRY NEIMAN
COUNSELOR AT LAW
51 EAST 42ND ST.
NEW YORK

Miss Celia Antopolsky
Passenger S. S. Alesia
Fabre Line—Piraeus—Greece

Oh my darling!

I wanted to come too—but I had promised myself not to, perhaps you know why, and just as I was about to break another resolution at 2:30 p.m. on the day, someone walked in on me and made me stay away. My sweet, I was at the boat too, in spirit, believe me. I wished you as much luck as the rest, kissed you a little more passionately and fervently, waved at you a little longer and wished as whole heartedly that you would not be away too long.

Five hours after you left we had a terrific thunderstorm, prolonged flashes of lightning and much rain. Celia dear, I hoped you were out of its area, and if not, that you were not as terrified as the women folk in my family, who huddled together in the living room, like sheep caught in a storm. Of course, I was the shepherd dog who quieted them—and what is more imp't, shut the windows. It lasted about half an hour and then cleared up so quickly one never would dream that only a very short time ago it looked like Machsheich's tzeit [Messiah's time].

I am glad you've started on another adventure—make the most of it (needless advice, you will)—write often—come back to us safe and sound to tell us all about it in your own inimitable way.

I follow instructions. Writing immediately after reading your letter, my regret is only that you can never guess with what gladness I read your letter, how happy and good to feel that you think of me—oh hell.

Good luck, bon voyage. Remember me to Lola [a nickname for Lillian].

Harry

Celia to Harry, September 18, 1930, writing on a lunch menu from the Alesia:

Harry, dear,

The sea is a shimmer of blue silk and white lace. The ship rides like some gallant steed from an old and vigorous legend, and the deck swings below my feet, and we eat and eat.

This is a customary menu, on which I am chancing a note, for the mail from the Azores, they say, is not safe, and may be delayed a long time. But I know you will like a memento, if only a wee one, from each city. The magical geographical dots are becoming amazing realities, and I know how you would glory in the looking forward to new scenes and new faces.

In the morning I study French in conversation with a ship's officer, and then I pace the deck; in the afternoon I study Hebrew with a Palestinian poet who has already written a poem to me! And then there's tea and talk; in the evening, dancing, or group singing or games, with the sea a dark surge and heave and the stars far away and sometimes, great moment!—the lights of another ship passing in the distance. My voice has come back splendidly, and I am happy. Much joy to you, dear boy, from

Celia

I go, for, at the moment, we are sighting land for the first time in five days. Write to Post Office, Tel-Aviv, Palestine. Write!

They went to a park, Harry remembered. They followed a paved walk over a low hill and as they descended she suddenly stooped to cup her hand around a white flower blooming beside the path. She looked up at him and said, "What a lovely thing!" And in her face he saw a spontaneous appreciation of all things beautiful, and he thought: *I'm going to marry this girl.*

He knew his family would not approve of his marrying a girl so unusual, so unconventional, a girl with no money, a child of immigrants not even from respectable Galicia, where his people came from, but from another part of Eastern Europe. He knew it and made his resolution just the same. His parents were judgmental and bound by tradition. They couldn't control his whole life!

Harry to Celia and Lillian, September 20, 1930

Address on envelope:
Misses Antopolsky and Shapiro
Passengers, S. S. Alesia, Fabre Line
Piraeus, Greece

–Last line crossed out, "*Marseille, France*" inserted
–"*Marseille, France*" crossed out, "*Poste Restante, Tel Aviv, Palestine*" inserted
–"*Tel Aviv*" crossed out, "*Jerusalem*" inserted

Miss Celia Antopolsky,
Miss Lillian Shapiro,

Gentle ladies,
Dear Girls,

I do not know when or where this will finally reach you, whether in Greece or in Palestine, but in either of those ancient places my ancient message will be in place—best wishes for a happy and profitable year in "de promis' lan'" —spiritually and aesthetically speaking, of course.

My love and hopes are with you both. Sincerely,

Harry

Harry to Celia, October 13, 1930

Celia, dear voyageure,

Your letter snatched me from this little room and with breathless speed took me to sea, to the Azores, Africa and the many fairy-like, dreamed-about, read-about places. Thank you for it, it was wonderful description! Is it any surprise that I had to leave this room and go for a long walk and feel sorry for being here, when there was so much to see and do in this world and so very little time to do it in and very little prospect of ever doing it? Of course, I soon consoled myself—came back with the resolution formed to make loads of "jack" and go myself—very soon—with you as guide. That's a resolution—not a promise. For some reason I feel so fidgety it's a hardship to write, all the more so because I feel that what will result is a poor thing beside the glowing beautiful thing I rec'd.

Celia, sweet, I'm happy that your trip really is becoming the beautiful thrilling adventure you planned and dreamed of so long, that you are living just as you are, doing what is nearest, dearest to you, seeing and feeling, not reading and wistfully sighing and hoping that some day in the future thus and thus will be—maybe—the devil of it all is that that future

24

is either too long in coming, or never comes at all. Motto: do it now.

Celia, I'm so envious I could cry. One thing is certain, I cannot write intelligently or legibly to-night—everything seems all tied up inside. Good-bye, I'll try again tomorrow.

I wait for your letters, anxiously and impatiently.

Love.
Harry

Regards to Lillian.

I can't enjoy my spaghetti without you. Now you'll surely understand.

Harry to Celia, October 19, 1930

My sweet,

Your letters come with such pleasing regularity and are so alive that I, too, feel myself one of the fortunate ones who can sweep everything aside and say—"excuse me everybody, I must go away for about a year or two and see whether my teachers were not spoofing me when I studied geography." Can you imagine, dear, what satisfaction to take the trip with you, eat spaghetti at Caruso's, sleep in my own bed (it's the softest in the world), make money hand over fist (I really am making about $40 per week average!) and pay nothing for it all!!! I'm a lucky stiff. But all that I rec'd, and all that I will receive, I owe to you, sweet girl. More power to that pen of yours.

When you left did you make due allowance for the cost of correspondence? I dare say it will amount to an <u>amount</u> by and by.

I've become a patron of the News Reel movie, for I don't want to miss you and Lillian. It's about time they awoke and did show us a few shots.

I've become acquainted with an honest to goodness Greenwich Village portrait painter, who is unique in that he is neat and clean and a real good business man. Perhaps that is why he cannot be a genius, but I am glad for geniuses make trying clients, though interesting girl-friends.

I hear so much about poets lately, that I am becoming uneasy. The King of Israel [an eccentric shipboard character Celia mentioned in her letters] I did not fear for I knew that you would be prejudiced because of his power, but a poor, unrecognized, young, handsome poet, ah, that is something to be approached with thought and action. I found some comfort only in the thought that I was far-sighted enough to send you a little picture of myself. Please, don't forget your little Galician in far-away America, "compare" as John David (the men's furnisher) would advise, see his eager whimsical face, the love in his eyes, the classic Grecian Galician profile! Surely no Palestinian will keep you away "not if you know values" (John David).

The picture you sent was a good one of you. You needed a hair-cut and had a broad smile on—the trip, then, has not changed you a bit. I'm glad.

I miss you, Celia.

Harry

Regards to Lola.

Chapter 5

Bullets in her bra

The hot air in the Casbah—the Old City in Algiers—was close, almost unbreathable, and yet there was comfort in the smells, the press of humans, the warmth, the pulse of life, as if the Casbah were a vast organism and the narrow, crowded streets its bloodstream in which Celia floated, free—for once—of any obligation to be outstanding or distinctive.

They walked uphill and down through narrow, sloping streets. An Arab man nudged past her and put his hand oh-so-briefly on her breast, cupping it, looking frankly into her eyes. An instant later he was gone, leaving her wondering whether she had imagined the encounter. There was danger in wide-eyed submission, in floating free. The locals never floated free: Their every move was colored by suspicion, tension, the awareness of danger.

Celia and Lillian had a mission in Algiers, an assignment; and in their big purses, with the straps slung diagonally over their shoulders and each purse pressed to its owner's side by a protective elbow, were bills of the multicolored Banque de l'Algerie currency that they had bought, surrendering good American dollars, from a money-changer at the dock. He had been lean, shrewd-looking, and tawny-skinned, and wore a faded tweed vest over his rumpled shirt and trousers. They had no idea of the exchange rates, but their new friend, Lev, said it was as good a deal as they were likely to get.

Winter in Palestine

A young woman's ideals and adventures in 1930

By Lillian Shapiro Marks

The article's caption reads: Lillian Marks experienced the life as a Zionist pioneer in 1930, from teaching shorthand and history in Jerusalem to posing with cattle at kibbutz Beth Alpha.

Excerpt from "Winter in Palestine: A young woman's ideals and adventures in 1930," by Lillian Shapiro Marks, **Jewish World, October 9-15, 1992:**

It was during our approach to Algiers that my friend and traveling companion Celia and I were asked by two Palestinians, a Jewish man and wife returning to their kibbutz [a collective farm], if we would each agree to smuggle a gun into Palestine for the defense of their kibbutz. The kibbutz had been attacked by Arabs during the riots of 1929, and guns with which the members had defended themselves were confiscated by the British. Guns and bullets could be bought in Algiers. The man expected to be searched thoroughly on his return to Palestine; his wife would be searched by body touch. She thought she would be safe in stacking bullets in her bra.

Celia and I agreed to bring the guns in. While the kibbutz members went shopping for guns, we bought cloth for sewing into holsters to attach to our thighs.

Lillian adds a clarification:

A Palestinian during the mandate period [the years when Britain controlled Palestine under a "mandate" from the League of Nations] was a citizen of Palestine, presumed to be a Jew. Most organizations which included the word "Palestine" were Jewish, such as the United Palestine Appeal, <u>Palestine Post</u>, Palestine Economic Corporation. Arabs living in Palestine called themselves Palestinian Arabs or just Arabs.

Throughout the 1920s, Arab resistance to the Zionists' presence became increasingly violent and well organized. The strategy of their leaders was to terrorize the Jews in order to drive them out of Palestine.

Eventually, over a one-week period in August, 1929, rioting occurred in Jerusalem and in various other parts of Palestine. During the Arab Riots of 1929, more than 400 Jews and 300 Arabs were killed or injured. Houses in Jerusalem were looted and libraries filled with irreplaceable books were burned.

But how does one ask a relative stranger to smuggle a gun under her skirt past military guards?

Lev was one of those short fellows whose chins were always tilted up as if in challenge. Although he couldn't have been older than thirty-five, his red hair was already thinning, perhaps because of his habit of constantly running his hand from front to back over his head. His weatherbeaten heavy pants and long jacket looked as if he wore them every day, which later turned out to be the case. His wife, Rosie, taller than he and very thin, wore a colorful scarf and had a ready smile that seemed to evidence joy in living, a quality Celia deeply admired. The two were both heavily tanned, yet there was something about them, an easy confidence in their movements, that seemed to brand them as American; that impression was confirmed when Celia overheard a few English words from the woman: "We must, somehow. We need them so badly."

They were returning from a visit to Lev's father, who lived in Boston and was old and ill.

"It was the last time," Lev said. "I'll never see him again alive."

"It must have been hard to leave him," said Lillian, her dark eyes sympathetic.

"It has brought him great happiness," Lev said, "to know that his son has returned to rebuild the homeland."

This was a different kind of Jew from those Celia had known. She could not imagine giving up her New York existence—her lively intellectual circle of friends, the chance of literary success—for some vision of technological miracles or of Biblical rural purity, in either case to be reached by years of physical labor amid sand and snakes and malaria. Nor would her parents have wanted her to do so.

"When we first came to Palestine, five years ago," said Lev, "we had no problem with the Arabs. They didn't bother us, we didn't bother them. Once I had a goat that wandered away and an Arab brought it back. When we had more wheat than we could eat, we shared with them.

"Then, after a year or two, we started having problems, little things. Sometimes an Arab would come into the kibbutz and just stand scowling and refuse to leave. The kibbutz was doing well and I think they started to envy what we had built."

"It's perfectly ridiculous, actually," Rosie put in.

Lev nodded. "Yes, there's plenty of room for Jews and Arabs to live side by side."

"Besides, we're helping them," Rosie said. "We're getting rid of the swamps, and that means more land and fewer mosquitoes. We're eradicating malaria. We're giving them jobs. We need workers, and they're happy for the work."

Lev said, "Trouble is, now they're organized. It's not as if we're just dealing with individuals. They all listen to their chiefs, or sheikhs, or whatever they call them. They're living in the past. They remember how before the War the Ottomans controlled all of Palestine. That's what they want back. They think if they can get rid of us, everything will be good again."

Rosie shook her head. "The fact is, it never was good for the ordinary people. They've always been poor."

"After the Arab Riots," Lev continued, "we went back to our usual routines. We took turns every night guarding the *kibbutz*. We heard that the British were studying the situation. We never did have any confidence that they'd be fair to the Jews. They've always sided with the Arabs. But then, before their study group even produced a report, British soldiers came and demanded that we produce all our guns. We did, and they took them. They confiscated our guns. Just like that!

"We tried to tell them we needed the guns to protect ourselves. But they just said, 'Sorry. We have orders.' I wish we'd hidden the guns."

Rosie said, "We're law-abiding people. It never entered our heads that they would leave us defenseless."

"The situation can only get worse," Lev said. "The Arabs and the Brits are both against us."

"So," Rosie said, "that's why we ask for your help."

Suddenly, the story was brought into the present.

After a buildup like that, they could hardly say no. Especially after they'd been telling their new friends about the adventures they'd had when they hitchhiked across America.

Of all their friends, Harry was the only one who might have said no, who might have told them to obey the law. But Harry wasn't there. And so, with the boat docked in Algiers, the conspirators separated. Lev and Rosie purchased the guns, while Celia and Lillian bought fabric, thread, and a good pair of scissors. The girls spent the rest of the day wandering in the newer parts of the city and imagining how it would be to live in one of the fine houses planted on hillsides overlooking the Mediterranean.

Back at the dock, they strolled up the gangplank with the innocent-looking fabric stuffed into their big traveling purses.

At dawn on October 13, 1930, they arrived at Jaffa, the Palestinian port. Though the Alesia was a very small ship, it was too big to approach the shore. It anchored off the coast and the passengers had to climb over the side of the ship and descend by rope ladders to waiting rowboats.

From "Winter in Palestine" by Lillian Shapiro Marks:

I was thrilled and fearful—thrilled to finally reach the Holy Land, a Zionist dream fulfilled, and fearful that the gun I had strapped to my thigh would be felt by the Arab oarsman who lifted each passenger from the rope ladder over the side of the <u>Alesia</u> down into his rowboat. On this sweltering day I wore a heavy tweed skirt to soften the feel of the gun.

Celia slipped on the wet edge of the ship and almost fell onto the oarsman, a tall, muscular young man. His face remained stolid as he caught her under her armpits and hoisted her up and then down into the rowboat. It was not an unpleasant experience, as she remarked to Lillian later, to be briefly airborne but securely held, rather like an earlier episode in which Harry, the lawyer, had rescued her from a minor calamity in the New York subway.

"Am I to spend the rest of my life being saved from mishaps by young men hefting me by the armpits? How undignified!"

After the *Alesia*, small as it was, the experience of being rowed in little boats by a ragtag bunch of Arabs felt absurdly primitive, as if the passengers and the rowers were merely children playing at visiting a real country. But after the girls were lifted onto the dock, the stern gaze of British customs officers in their khaki uniforms dispelled the illusion that this was a game. *They are just boys,* Celia told herself. *Like boys everywhere.*

The passengers formed a line for the mandatory body search. As they approached the soldier, a very young-looking blond Englishman, Celia and Lillian cast their eyes modestly downward, looking up shyly at him and smiling their prettiest, most winsome smiles.

"You're not—*really* going to search our *bodies*, are you?" They huddled together, putting their hands over their smiling mouths in mock terror, effective camouflage for their genuine terror.

The young man blushed and gestured to them to move on, skipping the body search. Success! They looked about for a porter to help with their steamer trunks.

But they faced yet another peril. Another officer, older and more stern-looking, pointed to a hand-lettered sign: HEALTH EXAMINATION REQUIRED FOR ALL PERSONS ENTERING PALESTINE.

A line of their fellow passengers had already formed outside a little stone building with a modern wooden door, painted brown, in which the mandatory health examination—whatever that was—was to be performed.

The girls approached the stern-looking officer.

"Couldn't we please come back and do this thing tomorrow?" Celia asked.

"Oh, please," Lillian said. "We're so tired, and it's so hot. We're not used to it the way you men are."

"You can see we're healthy," Celia teased, smiling up at him.

"We promise we'll come back tomorrow," Lillian said, wide-eyed.

"First thing tomorrow, before we do anything else!"

The two girls circled around him, smiling, until finally he said: "All right, all right. But mind you come back tomorrow to get the paperwork straight, or it's me who'll be in trouble."

"That is so *sweet* of you," said Celia, and the officer frowned and looked down at his feet.

"Just get out of here," he mumbled.

Chapter 6
Dear friend of a sudden meeting
*(Correspondence between Harry Neiman and Celia Antopolsky,
February 6, 1930 and November 1 to November 5, 1930)*

Harry had been well positioned near the train's sliding door when it opened. A woman in front of him got her heel stuck in the space between the platform and the train and began to fall, and Harry lifted her by her armpits up and into the train. They started to talk. He found her so charming that he stayed on past his station and got off where she did. He tried to walk her home but she refused, and so he asked her if she would go to dinner with him the following evening. She said she would meet him at the restaurant. Much later, she explained that she was ashamed of where she lived, because it was a poor neighborhood.

In the restaurant, she took off her hat and fluffed her curly hair to the way she usually wore it. He was embarrassed by her appearance; had her hair looked like that when he first met her, he would never have asked her out. But at dinner, she was as vivacious as before, and he already was determined not to give her up, no matter what his family and friends might say.

He liked to think of Celia as she was that first night, when he was behind her, lifting her up, his hands in her armpits—such an intimate posture, but necessary in the moment. He vowed that was what he would be to her in their life together, as if frozen in the pose. Harry, unimportant in himself—helping her, saving her, raising her up.

Celia and Lillian in Palestine

Letter from Celia to Harry on his birthday, February 6, 1930

Harry, dear friend of a sudden meeting, and of an afternoon on the side of a hill,

With the soft, cool wind that comes after a hot, restless day, I send you greetings on your birthday. I send them to you with swift strong wings, and with a joy in my heart like green leaves laughing to the sun.

These, also, are my gifts: awareness, with sensitivities reaching to the end of the earth and to the depth of any human spirit; understanding, with the gentle kindliness for always in your eyes; the great certain strength to be yourself, Harry Nieman [misspelled, should be Neiman] and no other; gladness in the joys of being and knowing and loving; beyond all things beauty for you, in every turn of your eye, in every thought of your mind, in every face you seek out, beauty, beyond all things.

The wind I send is heavy-laden, you see now, and smelling of spice. Lose nothing of it. All for you, glistening, dazzling, the gifts of this day, and for me, the thought that you are happy in them.

Sevia

Celia to Harry, November 1, 1930

Harry, my dear—

You don't know what a good feeling it is—or perhaps you do—to receive a letter in a strange country. It's like a warm handshake or like meeting you on Fifth Avenue as you turn into 42nd Street. I do wish I could give you part of my going, part of the joy I have in new places and new people, but you must stay fixed for a little while, just a little while and then you, too, will no longer "talk of going, but you'll be gone."

We are settled for the moment in Jerusalem where we have met several American acquaintances and have made many Palestinian ones. The city itself is wonderfully interesting with an old quarter very much like

Algiers, with Jews of every type and description walking about, from the pious Chassid with his long kaftan and his elegant side-curls to the brown Yemenites who are nearest to the Arab.

All about there are ruins and yet there is a constant building going on as if the aggressive ever-new wishes to wipe out the venerable, useless old.

It is quite customary to see a camel caravan bearing foodstuffs to the bazaars and it is also possible to be swallowed in a cloud of dust as the Hon. Mayor of Jerusalem whirls by in his Rolls-Royce. But the funniest sight of all is a great fat sheikh attired in all the flowing robes an Arab wears, going to see his veiled lady-love, perhaps, astride a tiny donkey that looks as if it were two by four inches. But these donkeys bear up nobly under the heavy loads imposed upon them.

Today, Jerusalem had the first rain in about six months—a half hour's heavy downpour and then a cold wet wind blowing. But, tonight, the Palestinian sky is alive again with stars and the moon is approaching the full. This is the first moon of my return and the second moon of my exile. "When I come to the land it will be a return." Write to me soon—everything!

Always—
Celia

Best regards from Lillian.

Harry to Celia, Saturday afternoon at the office, November 5, 1930

Dear Celia,

Please note the spelling of my name, the i comes after the e. Is it too late for you to change?

I met Joey Marks last Monday. He was looking well and still on the trail of "the interesting, yet lucrative job" (happy ideal) but has not found it as yet although at the moment I met him he was on the way to interview someone connected with the Jewish Telegraphic Agency in London and so it may be (here's hoping from this corner) that he has found it at last.

I suppose I ought to write something about the Poet and the Critic (The publisher mailed me one as soon as it came out. I've been considering what I should do about the subscription blank enclosed, for I really don't want to contribute to it, and whether it is the right thing to send him the cost of the copy he sent me)—something eulogious to please one of the contributors, but I won't. Is it tactless and stupid to say that I did not like it at all, that the getup of it was for the most part amateurish and, to me, uninteresting? Of course, I cannot very well read your contributions without being breathlessly interested and I honestly think your story was a very thick slice of life as lived in the sort of place and time of which you wrote. One or two of your poems seemed to me to be a little vague and I fail yet to know what you're driving at, perhaps that's my fault, not yours.

"Ellis and Joey loved your poems," Lillian said to Celia. "Everybody who's read them loves them. Harry just doesn't understand poetry."

"But why go out of his way to tell me he doesn't like them? Why not just keep quiet?"

"He must have thought you were waiting to hear from him."

"He seems so sweet, but reading his earnest letters makes me feel smothered and suffocated and sad. I think this man could suck the joy right out of me."

"You can teach him, Celia. Teach him to enjoy life. You can, if anyone can."

Top: *Religious Jews in Palestine*
Bottom: *The Wailing Wall in 1931*

Chapter 7

We know how to do this

A dream—a vision, a wish, a hope, an illusion, a fantasy, a willful dis-tortion of reality—however we might define it, the air in Jerusalem in 1930 was full of them.

As we have seen, Arab nationalists, infuriated by the breakup of the Ottoman Empire following World War I, dreamed of driving the Jews out of Palestine and building a new Arab state there, in what had formerly been a loosely defined region of the Ottoman Empire.

Jews from Europe had been settling in Palestine since the latter half of the 19th century, inspired by the movement known as Zionism, and driven by a desperate need to escape from Eastern Europe, where anti-Semitism was becoming increasingly virulent. In the Easter Pogrom of 1903, Jewish babies were said to have been torn apart by the bare hands of frenzied rioters. Some said the Russian government incited the pogroms; at any rate, the government took little action to stop them and encouraged the anti-Semitism that gave rise to them.

Many Jews fled to other countries, but those who chose to go to Pales-tine as Zionists believed that the Jews would never be safe until they had a land of their own.

While the Arabs and the Jews both dreamed of what they could do with the territory known as Palestine, that territory was controlled by

Britain under a "mandate" from the League of Nations.

The British Mandate was issued in 1922, but it tracked the language of the Balfour Declaration, a proclamation Britain had issued in 1917 in response to lobbying by wealthy British Jews. The Balfour Declaration read as follows:

"His Majesty's government view with favour the establishment in Palestine of a national home for the Jewish people, and will use their best endeavours to facilitate the achievement of this object, it being clearly understood that nothing shall be done which may prejudice the civil and religious rights of existing non-Jewish communities in Palestine, or the rights and political status enjoyed by Jews in any other country."

The Balfour Declaration had been greeted with joy by the Jews, who were dispersed throughout the world, primarily in Europe and America. They saw it as a promise that they would be allowed to return to the homeland from which they had been driven centuries before.

I imagine the British approaching the government of Palestine with confidence: *We know how to do this. We've done it before, all over the world.* They took charge right away, acting to prevent humanitarian disaster in Jerusalem after the war by restoring sources of food and medicines, repairing the roads as well as the railroad that had been dismantled by the Turks, installing pipelines and pumps to produce an adequate water supply, removing massive garbage heaps, covering standing water with mosquito repellent to eradicate malaria, and vaccinating the entire population against smallpox.

But the British did much more than manage the immediate public health crisis. They established government institutions and created a civil service. They designated Jerusalem as the capital of Palestine, hired a series of experts to draw up master plans for the city, and even decreed that all construction in the city was to use only "native Jerusalem stone," to preserve the city's distinctive appearance.

They also overhauled the Jerusalem sewer system, which dated back to Roman times; that project gave employment to both Lillian and Celia, as each of them worked for a time as secretary to the British engineer overseeing the project.

Many believe the British had no intention of ever turning Palestine over to the Jews, despite the terms of the Mandate, or to the Arabs, either; but rather that they intended to keep it as part of the British Empire.

The Jews didn't want only to restore their homeland in Palestine. They also dreamed of rebuilding their original, historic Jewish Temple, which had been located in Jerusalem's Old City on a hill, or "mount," known in English, as the Temple Mount.

The Jews had built the First Temple there in 957 B.C.E. During the sixth century B.C.E., the First Temple was destroyed by the Babylonians, but the Jews rebuilt in the same spot. The rebuilt version was known as the Second Temple.

King Herod, who ruled over the Jews as Rome's representative during the first century B.C.E., renovated the Second Temple and made major changes to the Temple Mount. He built massive retaining walls and filled in land as needed to create a large, flat area covering roughly thirty-seven acres, intended as a sort of platform upon which the Temple would stand.

The Second Temple was significant to Christians as well as Jews because it would have been the temple Jesus attended, from which he was said to have driven out the money-changers.

The Second Temple itself, although not the expanded Temple Mount on which it stood, was destroyed by the Romans in 70 C.E. To this day, religious Jews dream of the day when the Temple will be rebuilt.

But the Temple Mount was sacred to the Arabs, also.

There was a certain large stone on the Temple Mount. The Jews called it the Foundation Stone, and believed the First and Second Temples had been built over it. Jews regarded that stone as the spiritual junction of heaven and earth; in prayer they faced toward it. Muslims believed it was the place from which Mohammed ascended to Heaven during an event known as his "Night Journey."

In the seventh century C.E., Muslims built a shrine on the Temple Mount, precisely over the so-called Foundation Stone. This shrine was known as the Dome of the Rock, and its gold-covered dome dominated Jerusalem's landscape. Near it on the Temple Mount they built a large mosque, the Al-Aqsa Mosque.

Much of Jewish and Christian belief centered on the rebuilding of the Temple—who was to do it, when it was to be done, what its effect would be. The practical problem was obvious: The Temple could not be rebuilt unless the Dome of the Rock was destroyed first.

The "Western Wall" or "Wailing Wall" is actually a portion of King Herod's retaining wall, located on the western side of the Temple Mount. Traditionally, Jews gathered for prayer at that location because it was as close to the Foundation Stone as they could get, since the actual location was controlled by Muslims as part of a religious trust.

There were yet more dreams in Jerusalem in those days.

Religious Christians believed that the return of the Jews to Palestine was a necessary precursor to the Second Coming of Jesus.

Secular British citizens, on the other hand, were inspired by the *kibbutzim*, or collective farms, which were communes, based on socialist ideas. Many American Jews, including Celia and Lillian, were attracted to that vision of Palestine. The Jews on the *kibbutzim* were a different breed from the city-dwellers, sun-browned and accustomed to tough physical labor in the out-of-doors. It was said that a *kibbutznik* would work in the fields all day and play the violin or dance or talk philosophy all night.

The British struggled to manage the conflicts between Arabs and Jews.

The Jerusalem city government under the Ottomans had traditionally been Muslim, and the British continued that tradition, although by then Jews comprised a majority of the city's population.

The British selected Jerusalem's city officials from the upper-class, landed, educated Muslim elite in the Jerusalem area. In that group, two families or clans were traditional rivals. Both families were opposed to Zionism, but one of them tended to be more moderate and willing to compromise with the British and the Jews.

In 1920, after an episode of Arab rioting, the British removed the mayor of Jerusalem, who had been a member of the more anti-Zionist clan, and replaced him with a member of the more moderate clan. (That man was still mayor ten years later, when Celia and Lillian were in Jerusalem). To the Muslims, this event seemed to prove that the British administration was merely a puppet of the Zionists.

To reassure the Muslims, when another important office became vacant the following year, the British appointed a member of the strongly anti-Zionist clan to that position. His name was Amin al-Husseini.

From his position of power, al-Husseini deliberately fostered the hostility between Arabs and Jews regarding the Temple Mount and the Western Wall. He accused the Jews of planning to take possession of the Temple Mount and rebuild the Temple on the site of the Al-Aqsa Mosque.

Escalating hostilities regarding the Western Wall were the immediate trigger for the Arab riots of 1929.

After the 1929 Arab Riots, the Haganah, a Jewish self-defense organization, became much larger and came to include most of the Jews in the settlements and thousands in the cities. The Haganah sent representatives to Belgium, France and Italy to purchase arms and smuggle them into Palestine in suitcases and crates and—as we have seen—under the skirts of female Jewish tourists such as Celia and Lillian.

The 1929 Arab Riots led to a decision by some Palestinian Arabs to form an organization of their own that was anti-Zionist and anti-British. That organization, the Black Hand, was formed in 1930. In early April 1931, three members of a kibbutz near Haifa were ambushed and murdered by a militant wing of the Black Hand. News of the event quickly reached America, and Ellis mentions it in a letter to Celia on April 6, 1931 (see Chapter 21).

In the aftermath of the Arab Riots of 1929, Britain—confronted with its obvious failure to keep the peace in Palestine—appointed a commission to investigate the causes. The commission concluded that the fundamental cause of the riots was Arab fears "that by Jewish immigration and land purchases they may be deprived of their livelihood and in time pass under the political domination of the Jews."

Soon afterwards, Britain appointed another commission, headed by Sir John Hope-Simpson, to reconsider British policies regarding Palestine.

On October 21, 1930—just days after the *Alesia*, carrying Celia and Lillian, reached the Palestinian port of Jaffa—the Hope-Simpson Commission released its report and the British Government released a new White Paper, declaring that it no longer considered providing a homeland for the Jews as the central purpose of the Mandate. Jewish immigration into Palestine was to be severely restricted.

Chapter 8
The most stirring speech ever made
(Letters from Ellis Polonsky to Celia Antopolsky,
October 21, 1930 to November 18, 1930)

Harry, preoccupied with his law practice and his family's financial needs, was oblivious to the new British White Paper. Ellis, for a time, thought of little else.

Ellis to Celia, October 21, 1930

Marca—

"Back to your tents O Israel, back to your dwelling places O Jacob."

Israel has outlived Babylon and Rome and will outlive Great Britain. The swish of the tail of the Bull will not dismay the Lion of Judah.

Comerado, they have broken their pledge to us. These Gentiles have again been unkind to the Jews, we are panicky but not dismayed, hurt but not defeated.

Tonight again all of the people of Israel will raise their plaintive voice in protest—tonight all Israel will be One.

There is no mistaking the report from Great Britain. They have given prior claims to the Arab. The Arab who had his chance for two thousand years and did nothing—must now be placed and provided for before another Jew enters his home.

The aim they maintain is to build a Jewish Homeland—and the doors are closed to the Jews. "Home is a place where when you want to go there they have to take you in."

There is excitement and fever in Golus [Yiddish: Exile] but there is no weakness. You in Palestine know the emotion and determination at home.

Am Yisroel Chai [the soul of Israel lives]—

Ellis

Tonight at Mecca Temple a speech by Honorable Harry Snell M.P. will be replaced by a protest meeting—and I shall tell you of it.

E.P.

Ellis to Celia, October 23, 1930

Celia—

. . . When the news came, a sudden tenderness and helplessness touched our people. The Zionist offices were filled with Zionists, non-Zionists, Eastern Jews and Western Jews. It was like a family gathering at the parental home in the face of a tragedy . . . .

So the Jews protested in Mecca Temple. In less than a day's time a monster mass meeting. Thousands of incensed Jews were present—all of them with the same feeling of "well, we know it's not right but what can we do?"

Speakers spoke with spirited disapproval of the action and behavior of the Labor Government. The British Empire was booed and hissed.

The most dramatic moment came when Lipsky rose to speak. Aged and white from his efforts for Palestine, broken by the tragedies of his career, his being seemed to shriek, "For what have I gotten old? Was it all worth the effort and the struggle?"

But Marca, if you want to find one good reason for missing America, it is because you missed the most stirring speech ever made. John Haynes Holmes spoke with the fire of a prophet and with the wisdom of a sage. Time after time the Jewish audience rose to its feet to cheer, condemn and even to interrupt his speech with Hatikvah [Song, "The Hope," later to become the national anthem of Israel]. How I wish I could repeat it all to you.

"You Jews have learned your lesson, for twelve years you have lived in a Fool's Paradise. You wise people should have known that England or any other Imperial nation has no altruistic feeling and that the Balfour Declaration had no more value than any paper issued during the war." "If I were a hater of Jews, if I were a fanatical Arab, what would I do, I would close the doors of Palestine to them. If I were a hater of Jews, if I were a fanatical Arab, I would prohibit the sale of land—and this is what Great Britain has done."

How he inspired these people, how he comforted them, how he counseled them. He urged a cooperative movement between the Jews and the Arabs against England's Imperialistic policy. Not the resistance of force but the passive resistance of the Mahatma. It was so stirring as to lift up the heads of those who despaired and open the eyes of those who had been blinded . . . .

Today's paper gives us a ray of hope—a possible chance. The Tory Party led by Baldwin and Chamberlain announced their opposition to the Labor statement.

So we must choose a Baldwin in place of a MacDonald—a Conservative instead of a Labor party. But what's in a name—they're all politicians and the Jews must remain an issue to be fought about. May the Labor Party fall on the issue. Has God sent us a champion?

Am Yisroel Chai

Ellis

Ellis to Celia, October 28, 1930

Marca

Your very well restrained sentiments from Turkey have been received and I rush to convey to you my gratitude for your splendid offer of cooperation. In other words—your interpretation of the absence of mail at way ports was interesting and amusing. Did you really think a comerado could be just dropped out of one's life.

Of course, in the interim, I have made readjustments in the making of new friends and the fanning of embers into brighter and more vivid friendships. But, know this, silly child, that I have found you entirely unreplaceable and that whatever has or will happen can never really make me cold towards you. I miss you more frequently than I care to confess.

I am not unhappy, do not misunderstand me, but I have found that things in me that responded to things in you are unresponsive without you—and I know no matter what plans or adjustments I make, there shall remain in me a part of me that will be yours if you wish it.

Ultimately I begin to realize that I am not a unified personality that places an entire self into one mold. I am a multi-cellular being that offers in various manners parts of me that are stimulated to those that stimulate.

So say what you will and do what you will—whether I ever see you again or no—whether you reject or accept me I remain your comerado.

Enough of that—Hear ye—Walt Whitman has just been accepted into the Hall of Fame. Walt Whitman who had to be smuggled into the Hall by a group of intelligent students and placed face to face with poets of respectability who had called him uncouth—now will be ushered in with dignity and honor and placed with as much ceremony as those distinguished poets who mocked him. It's a holiday and I am proud of the man who gave me "comerado."

We still protest the Simpson report and the White Paper, and Sunday at Madison Square Garden we are going to hold an event on the 13th (hard luck) anniversary of the late Balfour Declaration. Here's hoping that MacDonald and his magnificent Labor party choke on the troublesome Jewish bone and he is thrown out by the Baldwin—Lloyd George group.

Your comerado,

Ellis

P.S. Conditions in good ole U.S.A. are awful—Jobs can't be had—millions unemployed. Psychologist exams will probably be given Jan. Have been asked to become Bklyn supervisor to clean up mess left by _____ who is still optimistic in search of success.

E.P.

Ellis to Celia, November 3, 1930

E. Polonsky
Young Judaea
111 Fifth Avenue
New York
U.S.A.

Marca—

A little note penned on Erev Shabbos [Friday, the eve of the Sabbath], brought a ray of Palestinian sunshine and a fresh spray of oriental wild rose. Then, you were my comerado and nothing else mattered. My Comerado had spent a moment with me and I was glad she was near.

I have lots to tell you of a mass meeting at Madison Square Garden, of 25,000 people who jammed the hall and of 25,000 who couldn't get in, of stirring moments, of brilliant speeches, of regained courage and pride.

I'll tell you all tomorrow.

My Land—my comerado.

Ellis

Ellis to Celia, November 4, 1930

Election Day—

It's a cold bleak day, Comerado, and the only warmth comes from thoughts of you—in a warmer and kindlier place. I am glad to feel that every day you are absorbing more and more the spirit and life of Palestine and that when you come back, if you come back, you shall return laden with fruits of love and devotion to our people and their home. There is no one whom I wanted Zionism to reach, more than you. I knew if you could be touched by Zionism, it would touch you more deeply than it could any one else. If there is any one thing I love my comerado for it is for her profound sensitivity, her unfathomable depth of appreciation and expression of beauty. I have found that depth present in no other person—nor do I expect to find it.

I heard some news and overheard other news from Marks. I understand you are now in Jerusalem, you have met Miller, Ehrlich and others; that you had been offered a year's teaching position and refused it because Lillian doesn't want to stay and that your new address is Jerusalem. I overheard Marks tell Harold [Lillian's brother] some news that I am sure would interest you. Marks had met your ardent admirer Harry Neiman and he seemed flushed with success and appears to be making over $100 a week. You'd better hurry up home and marry.

Please formally convey to Lillian my congratulations for the passing of her tests for teacher of shorthand and typing—and you dear comerado accept my hand for not having passed. Marks and Harold seem to be conspiring to have Lillian return before the new term begins, so she can be properly placed into harness and that it shouldn't be a total loss.

I think it would be a shame to return before having seen sunny Palestine greet the Spring and before having seen the offering of the paschal lamb [a lamb sacrificed at Passover] on Mt. Gerezin. Do not be swayed to return to bleak America until you have spent Passover in Palestine. Tell Lillian there will be enough substitute positions open if she returns in May—and at any rate she will be home and there will not be a pressing need for money. Once you leave Palestine, there is no telling when you'll get back.

I started this letter with the intention of telling you all about the great demonstration at Madison Square Garden but other thoughts pushed their impertinent way forward.

The meeting originally scheduled for 8 p.m. was filled to capacity by 7.15. It was all a lovely spectacle. Fish peddlers from Essex Street, tailors from the Bronx with their big buxom women, grey bearded scholars and taxi drivers all with the same indignant feeling towards a government which had been treacherous to their people. The Jewish Legion fell into a forgotten formation and marched militantly into the hall. Hundreds of young people banded together in groups that uttered defiant threats against a mighty empire.

A telegram from Borah, chairman of foreign relations committee, speeches by Hamilton Fish and Wagner, members of the committee, all condemned Great Britain and perhaps made really effective the protest. Mayor Walker, Felix Warburg, Prof. Frankfurter, and a number of others added their voices to the protest.

England will have to take back those words.

Shalom,
Ellis

Ellis to Celia, November 11, 1930

Marca—

"The greatest country of the world is Palestine and the greatest city in the greatest country in the world is Jerusalem . . . , thus said Halevi some 600 years ago and thus says my comerado some 16 days ago.

It is strange how I have made an adjustment and yet there is no adjustment. It's funny how I can go on for a day or so and feel perfectly adjusted and then comes my comerado to me through a sunset, through a friendly breeze, a clear moonlit night and even through a conclusive rain. It's strange how much more permanent and poignant thoughts of you remain.

And I am busy and becoming busier, all the time. Young Judaea has started and in Brooklyn I have found a sadly neglected and discouraged organization and I even have to accept the cooperation of D__[illegible name] in order to straighten things out. Today I have been chosen as editor of the Young Judaean Magazine for the month of December. I shall do this job incognito and the appointment will be kept secretive, for some reasons that are not worth explaining, but that will be a job, though an enjoyable one.

Election has come and gone in your Marcaless America and the Democrats have made a sweeping gain, protest of the people against Hoover and his bunk prosperity issue. But who cares?

America is proud and elated by the awarding of the Nobel Prize to Sinclair Lewis. One of the best plays on Broadway is Roar China, a Russian play depicting European tyranny over China.

Tell me of the country and of the girl that was My Marca. What does she think of and write about. How has her soul been touched?

Your comerado
Ellis

Ellis to Celia, November 14, 1930   Erev Shabbos [Friday]

Marca—

There's a rush in the Young Judaea office as there always is at this time of the day before Shabbos, but there's a comerado awaiting my "Good Shabbos" and the Bremen leaving tonight.

So—go little letter and tell her that I remember Fridays and they are sacred for a trip to the Palisades when I learned that Marca was beautiful, a Friday on which she presented me with a pipe over the candlelit table, a Friday on which we walked through a conclusive rain, a Friday which saw us riding mischievously (because I cut teaching) on the Third Ave. L—and more and more beautiful, happy, lazy Fridays.

I spoke to Marks and rebuked him for causing anxiety to Lillian. I didn't tell him that you knew what he had written. I shamed him and told him he ought to be more considerate and suffer if he has to, alone. I told him how much she gave up to take the trip and he was helping to spoil it. He admitted that he had written some depressing letters but he has written more cheerful ones lately.

Tell her Marks is doing well and is lonely only when he writes, he just wants sympathy. He has enough to do and enough people to socialize with to keep him busy. Tell her that she flatters herself to think that he needs her so much. Be the strong one, comerado and I shall be proud that my comerado is sturdy.

Shalom, comerado

Ellis

Ellis to Celia, November 18, 1930

Marca

To mind comes a rather half remembered piece of a beautiful bit that has made my comerado my comerado.

"Thru a day of littleness, the thought of you careens

Like a splash of gold on a patch of mental greens."

It doesn't sound accurate to me but that is how the victim feels towards the author.

Unaccustomed as I am to consistent detail work, a few hours of it tires me and bores me. It is then that the thought of you and a word to you lifts me from the monotony of it all—or what's a comerado for.

I am working with a vengeance handling a half dozen jobs and a great deal of work ahead. Editing the Young Judaea magazine means writing the magazine. Everything from the serial to the puzzles, from the editorial to the news etc. If you would see what they have made of your lazy comerado, you'd weep tears of sympathy.

Today came the report of the result and reports of the Parliament debates on the Palestine question. The stirring talk and vitriolic attack on the Labor Party by Lloyd George, the speeches of Amery and Samuel are interesting and encouraging, the apologetic answer of MacDonald weak— but the net result disappointing and discouraging.

In spite of all this there is little to tell you of New York. This week I probably felt your absence most poignantly (pronounced poiñantly) because I picked up threads of supervision in Brooklyn and passed by and into painfully reminiscent places.

I passed a park near Utica and Eastern Parkway and there came the realization that that was the park we walked through with Tyl and Lillian one night after a party, a party that was disappointing because there were too many people paying attention to you. And I wanted this week to walk through the park with you arm in arm.

And I went to the H.E.S. [the Hebrew Educational Society], the birth-place of our comeraderie, and I saw the rabbi and the office and the same desks and I felt your absence. And I spoke to the new club directress, a very efficient and stern but pleasant young lady and we spoke all evening just as we used to do—and I left feeling that I spoke to her in order to fill a need for you and it was all unsatisfying.

Comerado
Ellis

Excerpt from the **Bulletin of the National Conference of Jewish Charities:**

The new building of the Hebrew Educational Society of Brooklyn was dedicated on Sunday afternoon, June 7th [1914]. It is located at Hopkinson and Sutter Avenues, [in] Brownsville . . . .

The building includes an auditorium with a gallery having a capacity for 500 persons, a gymnasium below the auditorium and a roof garden above. On the first floor are the administration offices and social room.

On the two floors above there are fifteen club and class rooms, including one for Hebrew, three for music and one for domestic science. In the basement are a men's social room, showers and lockers for the gymnasium . . . . Part of this plot is not occupied and will be used for the present as a farm garden.

The new Hebrew Educational Society Building represents the first completely equipped structure established by a private organization for the purpose of a Jewish social center in Brooklyn. It caters to the largest homogeneous population in that borough. The Brownsville district is assumed to contain about 150,000 Jews.

CHARLES S. BERNHEIMER,
Superintendent

A street in the Old City in Jerusalem

Chapter 9
If an Arab approaches you menacingly
(Lillian Shapiro's impressions of life in Jerusalem)

Excerpts from "Winter in Palestine: A young woman's ideals and adventures in 1930," by Lillian Shapiro Marks, **Jewish World, October 9–15, 1992**

. . . Our ride to Jerusalem in an old car shared with other passengers was on a narrow, winding road with hairpin turns called the "seven sisters." The land on each side was light tan and rocky, with an occasional fenced-in area of small pine seedlings planted by the Jewish National Fund. We were told that the Arabs' herds of goats ate any tree sprouts that emerged. We passed a field being cleared of rocks, one by one, to create a stone fence around a field to be cultivated. The soil looked dry and sandy . . . .

Celia and I checked into Warshofsky's Hotel on Zion Square. The traffic on Jaffa Road consisted of occasional cars, occasional camels and some horse-drawn wagons . . . At sunset fellaheen (Arab farm workers) trudged with wooden plows home from plowing the fields of absentee Arab landowners.

The Zion Cinema not only showed films but was also used as a concert hall. When a fine musician. . .performed it was possible for those who could not afford a ticket to hear the music by sitting on the ground, leaning against the back of the building. When one saw a film in the Cinema it was wise to be surrounded by friends, on the side and in the rear. Otherwise, one might find oneself pinched on the rear by a friendly Arab.

There was no public transportation in Jerusalem. We walked everywhere. Most private houses had a wall surrounding a garden. Rehavia, a brand new neighborhood, consisted of one unpaved street and a few houses. With the lack of water and trees, except for olive trees, migrating birds bypassed Jerusalem. In their absence the donkey with its raucous braying was called the Jerusalem nightingale.

The Old City was romantic. There was no electricity. The shops were lit with oil lamps. To make a purchase one needed to know the fine points and nuances of bargaining. There were beggars at every turn who asked for baksheesh and Arab boys who offered their services as guides . . . .

After a few days spent in becoming acquainted with Jerusalem, it was time to find work. Both Celia and I had taught in a New York City high school and left with letters of recommendation from the principal. We also had secretarial skills. Among the letters of introduction we carried was one to Gershon Agronsky (later Agron, the mayor of Jerusalem), the editor and publisher of the <u>Palestine Post</u>. A telephone call to him resulted in an invitation to his Friday night open house. Here Mr. and Mrs. Agronsky brought together the English-speaking Jerusalemites. They knew all the news of the community.

Thus we were told that the senior English mistress of the Evalina de Rothschild School was called back to England because her mother was ill. A supply teacher (a substitute) was needed for this girls' elementary and high school supported by

British Jews. In addition, teachers of English were needed at the Alliance Israelite, at the adult Hebrew evening high school and the Teachers' Seminary.

[I was hired to teach at the de Rothschild School.] Celia taught English at the Teachers' Institute. English textbooks were scarce, but the students had been studying Shakespeare. On Celia's first day a student wanted permission to go to the lavatory. She asked, "Prithee, my teacher, wilt thou grant me a boon?"

When I substituted in the evening high school, the only textbooks available for the beginning English class were Tolstoy's Fairy Tales . . . .

I learned how involved each Jew in Palestine was with the life of the country. Gradually, even I felt the fullness and excitement of two kinds of existence, a personal one and a national one. Every bit of news was important—the British White Paper limiting Jewish immigration even though Arabs were free to enter Palestine at every border, the arrival of a ship with illegal immigrants smuggled in at the beach during the night, the discovery of an ancient synagogue floor while plowing, the advances Hadassah was making in combating trachoma which accounted for the number of blind Arabs being led through the streets by young boys.

With a group of Americans of my age, discussions were lively. We met at Patt's bakery and garden restaurant on the Street of the Prophets, where Mrs. Patt mothered us. Sometimes we met at the Vienna Café, where one spoke cautiously because a stout patron was pointed out as a spy, now for the British, formerly for the Turks.

Emma Ehrlich, the devoted secretary of Henrietta Szold, the founder of Hadassah, and later of Youth Aliya [emigration to Israel], acted as big sister to American young women in

Jerusalem .... Emma informed us as to what was and what was not acceptable behavior for a young Jewish woman in Jerusalem. I learned that my innocent dancing with a British officer at a tea dance in the King David Hotel was unacceptable. At this time the British were regarded as enemies.

Saturday mornings we often went on a <u>tiyul</u> (a hike) to Bethlehem, keeping in step as we sang Hebrew songs. We passed shepherds playing their flutes and shielding baby lambs in the upper folds of their garments. On the rare occasion when a friend could have the use of a car, we piled in and drove down to the Dead Sea.

We had to observe two restrictions. The first was in the use of water, which was scarce. Taps could be turned on for only two hours a day. Water had to be hoarded. It was said with some exaggeration but with a core of truth that a good Jerusalemite first used a given amount of water for cooking, then for washing dishes, then for bathing, then for washing clothes, then for washing the floor and finally for watering the garden.

However, when a winter rain came, it descended with great force as if the heavens had opened ... Then just as suddenly as it had started, the rain stopped .... The parched fields immediately blossomed with red anemones and a profusion of bright wild flowers.

The second restriction was based on the fact that it was not safe for a European or American woman to walk without an escort in the Old City or anywhere after dark. This was difficult for me since I was accustomed to the freedom of New York where, believe it or not, it was safe for a young woman to go anywhere day or night, whether in the subway or Central Park at midnight.

Lillian to her brother, Harold Shapiro:

Monday, December 29, 1930
Jerusalem

Dear Harold,

In a few days, you reach the grand anniversary of your birthday—27 years. A few years ago, it sounded old, but now it sounds very funny. My heartiest congratulations and best wishes of every kind for you. And wake up, Harold—remember that even though you are 27 yrs young, your sister wants to hear from you. It is almost two weeks since your last letter came.

Christmas day came with a collection of American and English tourists and some additional church bells. In Bethlehem, a midnight mass was preceded by a procession of monks and priests. I did not attend the services because I hear that the Greek Orthodox put on a better show for their Christmas, in about a week.

Last night, for the first time, I went through the old city after dark. It was a mystical experience. A dull half moon gave a vague, diffused light, and long streets of stairs had overhanging arches and balconies that had the look and odor of ages gone by. Celia and I had ample protection of five men, including Marcus Kramer. Our escorts knew every stone of Jerusalem, and knew the Biblical and historical significance of each point. The atmosphere is such that the historic anecdotes seem more than likely to be real.

We came out of the Gate of the Lions at the other side of the city and walked past the supposed Gethsemane, which is fertile with olive trees. Arab villages twinkled in the distance. We walked along the road to Jericho, but turned off into the valley of Jehoshaphat, and up again to the wall of the city which we mounted and walked along, in the manner of those who watched from the walls for the approach of strangers or enemies . . . . Once more within the city, we were told of the conditions at the time of the Turks. Then, in the new city, we completed the experience with

Turkish coffee at midnight. Only Jerusalem could be as fascinating just by walking through it.

I am sending you a buya (I have no idea how it is spelt) [she means an abaya]. It is a cover-all robe which the Arabs use for everything from an outer garment to anything it may degenerate into. Jews use it for dressing-gowns. Take your choice!

I am teaching this week at the de Rothschild School, substituting.

Celia has not yet heard from Pater regarding any argument or check. He is suspiciously silent.

How is the Bank of the U.S. faring? How much have we in it?

Celia also sends her best wishes to you for your birthday and otherwise.

Love to the family.

Lillian

The notation on the outside of the package is to ward off Customs Officials.

More excerpts from "Winter in Palestine: A young woman's ideals and adventures in 1930"

. . . I then became secretary to a British engineer who had come from work on the Aswan Dam in Egypt and was now to reconstruct King Solomon's water system into the drainage system of Old Jerusalem. He had two offices, one on Mamila Road in the new city and one overlooking the Mosque in the Old City . . . .

There was an air of excitement in the office in the Old City. Workers brought in artifacts dating to biblical times that they dug up. They discovered the remains of bridges and aqueducts mentioned in the Bible.

On the days that I worked in the Old City office a body-guard came to my lodging and, ten paces behind me, followed me to work. He was black, more than six feet tall, brightly turbaned and pantalooned with a sword in his sash. He looked as if he came out of an illustration from an Arabian Nights Tale. I called him my genie. He never spoke. At the end of the work day he followed me home . . . .

During Hanukkah vacation Celia and I hitchhiked through the Emek [the Jezreel Valley, a fertile plain]. Emma advised us, "If an Arab approaches you menacingly, kick him in the groin." We welcomed the wonderful green around the settlements in the Emek. Everywhere we found warm hospitality. We helped with work. We took part in lively discussions after work. There was always singing and dancing at night . . . .

It was time for me to return to New York . . . Handing over my job with Mr. B. to Celia, I said my farewells . . . .

Lillian and Celia

Chapter 10
They knew they couldn't stop us

L illian Shapiro's mother had died in a fire that destroyed the family home in 1913, when Lillian was seven years old. Lillian and her older brother lived with relatives for a year until the family persuaded her father to marry a woman they found for him, to provide a home for himself and the children.

At first, the new Mrs. Shapiro was kind to the children. But soon that changed and she began to terrify the children with furious rants. Mealtimes were silent and strained. Lillian learned to be as unobtrusive as possible.

At the beginning of the tenth grade at Girls' Commercial High School, the quiet, serious, still-grieving girl met Celia Antopolsky and was immediately drawn to her because of her name: Lillian's mother had been named Celia. Lillian and her new friend Celia were both bright and especially talented in English. While Celia loved to be the center of attention and thrived on the admiration of others, Lillian was happiest staying in the background, giving support, planning, solving problems before they arose, and sincerely admiring Celia for her talents.

Celia lived in a rambunctious, noisy household, filled with family and friends coming and going, the sounds of musical instruments—piano, tuba, fiddle—and the competing smells of Mama Antopolsky's bread for her bakery business and the turpentine for Papa Antopolsky's paint business. An extra friend for dinner or even to spend the night posed no problem, and soon Lillian was practically living in the Antopolskys' house.

The two girls did everything together. That first year, when they were only 16, they used a vacation school break to hitchhike to Montreal, to visit a friend who had moved there. It was the first of their many hitchhiking trips. Many years later, I asked Lillian how they got their parents to agree to let them make that trip, and she said, "They knew they couldn't stop us. We would do whatever we wanted."

Both girls were admitted to New York University, but the University was willing to give only one scholarship. Lillian suggested she and Celia share it, making up the balance with part-time jobs, and the University agreed; Lillian told me those were the first partial scholarships the University had ever granted. When Celia ran for vice president of the freshman class, and won—the first woman ever to hold that position—Lillian was her "campaign manager."

In college, Celia was the center of a group of artists and poets, reminiscent of the Paris salon of Gertrude Stein and Alice B. Toklas, which flourished at approximately the same time. Friends called the group the MacDougal Street Salon; they probably gathered at one of the cafés on MacDougal Street, which was located just west of Washington Square and so was convenient for New York University students.

After they had graduated from New York University and hitchhiked across the country and back, Celia and Lillian together created another literary salon in a tenement apartment at 400 Madison Street, on the Lower East Side of Manhattan. Lillian's father owned the building and let the girls live in it rent-free.

Celia capitalized on the experience by writing a humorous article about breaking the news to her parents. It was published—under a pseudonym and with facts slightly disguised—on the front page of the "English Section" of the *Forward*, a Jewish newspaper, on February 24,

1929. The article was called, "THERE'S NO PLACE LIKE HOME—BUT ONE'S OWN STUDIO IS BETTER," with two subtitles: "This is the Story of a Jewish College Girl Who Scandalized Her Parents by Moving Into a 3-Room Cold Water Flat on Madison Street," and "Lots of Jewish Business and Professional Girls Prefer to Live Away From Their Families And We Hardly Blame Them."

Celia and Lillian painted the three small rooms themselves, working in secret (that is, without telling Celia's parents) night after night. Papa Antopolsky was in the business of painting houses and selling paint, and the girls probably "borrowed" from his inventory in the basement of the house on Liberty Avenue, in Brooklyn, where Celia still lived with her family.

> We played with the apartment as if it were a doll's house. Finally, the dull walls entirely disappeared and we had a living room with walls of green and woodwork the color of apple blossoms, a kitchen in orchid and yellow, a bedroom in blue and cream. We gradually bought some bits of furniture, bright cretonnes, lamps, cushions, and vases. We were ready to live in the rooms we had lovingly built for ourselves . . . and still I had not told my family.

She describes the desire for a place of her own as grounded initially in frustration at the lack of privacy in the Antopolsky household, but . . .

> During my sophomore year, a new phase introduced itself to the situation. I wrote a poem or two and became one of the artistic group in the college. I associated now with lean, pallid youths and Madonna-faced or mad-haired girls who had all been brought up in good Jewish homes but who languidly pretended to be neo-Greek and utterly abhorrent of bourgeois manners. I dreamed now of a literary salon . . .

According to Celia's article, her parents, after much argument, were mollified when she described the apartment as an "office" in which she could do her work while theoretically continuing to live at home, thus saving them the shame of admitting that their daughter, a single woman, had moved out.

Mr. Shapiro had a business reason for letting the girls live in the building. He hoped their presence would attract other young people, and that proved to be the case.

Among those attracted were Ellis Polonsky and Joey Marks, who roomed, with another young man, in the flat directly above the girls. "The Apartment," as the girls' flat was called by its devotees, became a hangout for young people interested in art, literature, or politics, and also for a young lawyer named Harry Neiman, who was interested in Celia.

While living in the Apartment, Celia and Lillian supported themselves by teaching shorthand and typing at their old high school, the Girls' Commercial High School in Brooklyn. Neither had a teaching license yet, but the principal thought highly of them and was sure they would pass the qualifying test. They continued teaching through the spring of 1930. After the school year ended, they were able to squeeze in summer jobs in a children's camp before the trip to Palestine.

As it turned out, Lillian passed the teaching test but Celia didn't. But by the time the results came out, the girls were already on the way to Palestine. Despite the economy, they were confident that the good times in the Apartment had been only a foretaste of how their lives would be when they returned.

Chapter 11

Station IKE

(Correspondence between Celia Antopolsky and her family,
November 14, 1930 to February 12, 1931)

Irving Antopolsky, Celia's younger brother, to Celia, November 14, 1930

This is Station IKE broadcasting from the Antopolsky Circus, well known on Liberty Ave., and located in the choicest part of East New York, only a stone's throw from Chaimowitz's Candy Store and but a short distance from Cohen's the home of dry goods. No doubt, ladies (and gentlemen), you might be interested in a brief description of the Circus, and in how it functions. Nothing is more pleasant to us than obliging you. The Antopolsky Circus was founded by one Aaron David, a large man with a flair towards the dramatic. He, incidentally, is the man with the loud voice, whose tales of woe you no doubt have greatly enjoyed in his previous broadcasts. He is, today, at the age of 62, in remarkable health and fine lung power. Now ladies, etc., let me tell you of the driving force behind this circus, who is the wife of Aaron David, and manages the show. Among her many accomplishments, she boasts of being the mother of four children, whom I will describe later in the program. You may be interested in knowing that at present she is a healthy fine woman whose hobby is one Joanie, whom I shall later describe in detail.

One moment please, for Station Announcements and the correct time. When the gong sounds it will be exactly 10.30 p.m. in the Anto Circus. "Gong."

The show begins, folks, with a rather unique setting, the entire play taking place in the rear of a paint store, the date being Nov. 12, 1930, and the entire circus present, the audience being composed of many people, among whom are present representatives of the Cohen, Siegel and Blum families. The Antopolskys, or I should say the cast, are all feeling fine, business being passable, peace having reigned for a while, and the son of the family in deep if fanciful contemplation over the problem of whether to take the touring car or the sedan for the date Sat. Nite. Conversation is usual and the play opens with the star actress, Madame Joan Feirtag, entering the room.

Bear with us just a moment, dear members of the radio audience, while your announcer goes out to see whether he has a flat tire or it was just an ordinary explosion. Thank you and now

Aaron David—<u>Ich zug dir az es lant zich nit hurven far azane pascuni-aques.</u> [Yiddish. Translation: I'm telling you, it doesn't pay to work so hard for such S.O.Bs.]

Sarah (Wife)—<u>Emes, Aren David, mi git zee essen un trinken un shluffen, un az men bet zee untzushreiben a letterr tzu Tzivie, villen zee nisht. Alevei vet yich gekeut shreiben. Vet yich zee getzeigt</u> [In truth, Aaron David, we give them (make it possible for them) to eat and to drink and to sleep, and if we ask them to write a letter to Celia, they don't want to. If only I could write. I would show them].

Joan enters

Aaron David—Hello Jonetal, whose girl are you?

All at once:
Uncle Ike [Irving]—Who do you love, Mama's Isie or Baba's Isie?
Grandma Sarah—<u>A leben aff mein kindele</u> [Life (blessings) upon my child].
Miss Gump [Minna]—Sing, Joanie, and I'll dance

Madame Feirtag [Betty]—Upstairs; you gotta go to sleep or I'll cripple you

Nathan Feirtag—Irving, give me a butt, will ya, I'm all out of cigarettes

Joan (heroine)—with expression and look of pain—"I wanna make"—
Excitement.

Curtain ends excitement

And now ladies of the radio audience, if you have enjoyed our little offering this evening, write and let us know. If the demand is great enough, we will have the same cast at a later date play that never ending comedy drama "Poker on Sunday afternoon" starring the famous Isaac Goldberg, ably supported by the Rabbit and equally well known players.

And so, before going to bed tonight, folks, remember that Antopolsky's turpentine smells stronger than all the rest, and also, if you must ruin your house by painting yourself, use Antopolsky's paint.

This is Station IKE, the voice of Liberty Ave., now snoring off. Bidding you a fine adieu until the next postscript—

P.S. all kidding aside, everything home is jake. The radio story is true to life. I'm doing pretty well at law school, having passed both conditionals taken in the summer. Glad to hear you're enjoying yourself, and look forward to your letters. Write often, and long letters, the longer the better. Regards from all to Lillian and yourself, and best wishes from your brother

Irving

P.P.S. Joanie celebrated her third birthday last week and kept asking for you. Send her congratulations and if possible, some sort of inexpensive gift. Anything you think she'll get a kick out of.

Well so long.

Celia Antopolsky to her older sister, Betty Feirtag, November 22, 1930

Dear Betty,

You have no idea how much I enjoyed receiving your letter. If you had you'd sit down at once and write another. It was the first news I had had from home and I really had been terribly worried. In fact, I was going to send a cable when I saw the welcome Liberty Avenue address.

Please ask Mama and Papa, as well as everybody else, not to worry at all if they do not receive letters with great frequency. The mail is very uncertain at best, and besides I have been very busy here. I secured a job teaching English in the Mizrahi Seminary for Girls. These girls, from 15 to 19 years of age, are a most interesting lot, alive, intelligent, and full of fun. They're way ahead of American students who are utterly colorless by contrast. You should hear them babble in Hebrew. And their imaginations! Untainted by the stupidity of the News and the Mirror.

Jerusalem itself is like a city in a dream. To walk along a street is to imagine yourself in the pages of the Old Testament. The donkeys still roam about carrying great loads, as such transportation is still cheapest and most convenient. There is no funnier sight than a fat Arab sheikh (note spelling!) on a tiny donkey. It is also a common sight to see a long string of camels laden with produce coming out of the desert. The motor car, while it is becoming more and more common, is still a luxury. The result is that after eight o'clock in the evening, the city is dead quiet. You cannot imagine such silence, you Antopolsky-Feirtags. Yet all the peace in the world seems concentrated in the Jerusalem hills.

Jerusalem is no place to make money. All the people are poor. They have no steam heat, no silk stockings, no evening dresses, no theatres except perhaps a movie once a week. But they have a beautiful sun for ten months of the year, they live in large airy rooms, they have gardens, they never hurry, there are no streetcars and no subways and almost no telephones. They scarcely miss money, except, of course, some of the young boys and girls who have never left Palestine and think that America is a Paradise on earth. If one comes to Palestine with American money, one finds that it has exactly double value. You can build a house here for $2,000 and a family can live for $60 a month.

Just now, it is cold here and I am very thankful for all my warm clothing. But spring comes again in February and even now, after the rain, the flowers are beginning to appear, the trees are green and sweet-smelling, and I walk along in the bright sun feeling that the world is mine. Someday, I should like Mama and Papa to come here to live but I should like them to be supported by American money.

It is really very necessary to know Hebrew here as everyone speaks it. I am just beginning to understand. The old Jews, of course, the ones who came here to pray and to die, still consider Hebrew the holy language and continue to speak in Yiddish. But business and social life is all carried on in modern Hebrew.

I find that, in the quiet life here, I am able to write very well. In fact, the whole life here seems taken out of a novel.

We are planning to work on a kvutzah [kibbutz] or colony for a month or two, but that is nothing at all when you think of those who suffered all the tortures to escape from Russia to Palestine, and then gave their youth to the building of something where there was nothing before. We are really playing at Palestine where these people are living it.

I am glad to hear that Mama is better. I really miss her sometimes very much and when I visited Rachel's tomb I silently offered a prayer that she be well for many years to come. If prayers go to heaven, surely from that place they have special delivery.

How is Papa feeling? Give him my love.

I wish I had time to write at length to everyone, but it is almost impossible. Tell Irving that I received his letter and almost rolled off the bed laughing at it. Lillian too. His letters are more than welcome. Tell him to write again, that I shall answer soon, and that I am overjoyed to hear that he is doing well in school. I have implicit faith in his ability.

I wish Minna could come here, if only to see what it means to be a Jew, if only to hear the young boys and girls sing their modern Hebrew songs. It's a new life and a real one that they have here.

Best regards from Lillian to all. Please write soon to

Your sister
Celia

Mama Antopolsky to Celia (written for her by Betty), December 30, 1930

My dear daughter,

I had been awaiting a letter from you anxiously, and when it finally did arrive, it certainly delighted us all.

I am glad to know that you like Palestine so well. From your description of Jerusalem, there is no doubt that the place must be beautiful. Believe me, I wish I could go out there to live. The climate, no doubt would do me a world of good, as I do not feel the way I should lately. Just what do you intend to do? How long do you expect to stay abroad. I wish you would write and let me know.

We all miss you a great deal. Even though you weren't home so often, I always did look forward to your home coming on Friday evening. I also miss the little bouquets of flowers. Now it is kind of quiet here. Irving I believe is love sick. He washes his neck very often lately. I am not sure, but I think his heart is affected. I do not know the girl but there is a rumor that her name is Flo, and that she is a school teacher, and that she is a blonde. I believe that is where he is getting his sudden ambition to work at his studies.

Minnie is still entertaining her old flame, regardless of battles and lectures, etc. [Minna's "old flame," Al, was not Jewish.]

Joanie is the only ray of sunshine here. She is too sweet for words. An adorable little devil. She has grown quite a bit and speaks lovely. She hasn't forgotten your send off and is always reminding us of Celia that went on the boat.

As usual there is the Sunday evening reunion playing poker downstairs. It's a lucky thing Papa can play cards, otherwise we wouldn't know our family.

C____ W____ is getting married Mar. 1st to none other than Sadie's brother Dave Rubin. It was a case of love at first sight. They are both dumb so it's OK.

A fellow by the name of Bill called and wanted to know your address.

Also your lawyer sweetheart phoned to find out whether we heard from you or not.

Lillian's father paid us a visit. He has it in for you two for taking the trip. You see, Lillie's diploma came and he felt bad because she couldn't be here now to hold her job. Yours did not get here. I do not know why but I believe you didn't pass the test.

There has been a run on the Bank of the United States and it has been closed. Sholem had his money there. He had been depriving himself of even necessities so that he might be able to bring over his family from Europe and now all his hopes and dreams are shattered. He had about one thousand dollars there.

Celia, do not bother looking up Morris's Aunt, as I have heard that she passed away two years ago.

Keep well and write as often as possible. It is the hardest thing for me to get someone to write a few lines. Lots of love and best regards from all to Lillian and you.

Mother

P.S. Mama insisted on having this letter written to you from her so it goes for me too. I had to laugh when you wrote that at 8 o'clock you take the sidewalks in. We haven't gone to bed before 2 o'clock a.m. for the last month.

Minna Antopolsky, Celia's younger sister, to Celia, January 8, 1931

Dear Celia,

Your letters are certainly a revelation to Mother, Papa, the family, the relatives and the neighborhood.

Everybody is O.K. here. The panic did not affect us directly but a great many Brownsville people were affected by the closing of the Bank of the United States. Our cousin Sholem had all the money that he was saving to bring his family here, in one of the branches. Papa didn't have any of his money there. But business is punk and it's been a rotten winter here.

But we are glad that we're all well because there's some kind of a throat disease that's going around in New York. It's an influenza of the throat. So we're all being very careful not to catch colds.

Mama says that she feels that she sees you every time one of your letters comes. She talks about you every day and wants to write every week, if only a post card.

About two months ago, I had the pleasure of meeting your boy friend Harry Neiman. He is very interesting and I spent a very nice hour or so with him. You see, he sent us a picture of you in Athens that he thought we would be interested in seeing, and he asked us to return it, at our convenience. So, one afternoon I went up to see him. And you don't have to worry about whether I made an impression or not. I know I did. He asked me to come again and have lunch with him, but I got a job right after that at R. H. Macy's in the advertising dept. and worked until Xmas so I didn't go. I gather that Harry is very sweet on you. I'll tell you all about it when I see you. Anyway, if you permit me to voice my opinion, I would say that I think he would make a very nice brother-in-law.

C_____ W_____, who is staying with us, is going to marry Dave Rubin, Sadie Rubin's brother, if you know him. A Canadian girl gets Hinsdale Street's best catch. A plumber, making a fairly good living.

(Confidentially) Brother Ike has a girl and I hear she's very nice. Result: Irving gets up mornings.

Best regards to Lil from Mom, Pop and the rest incl. Joanie.

Love,

Minna

Mama Antopolsky to Celia, January 8, 1931, written by Minna and enclosed with Minna's letter:

Beloved Daughter—

What you write about Palestine leads me to think that it is a wonderful place to live in. Will you let me know the practicality of our family settling in Palestine for good?

From

Your loving Mother

Betty Feirtag (née Antopolsky) to Celia, February 12, 1931

My dear Celia,

We have just received a letter from you, and believe me it was about time you did write. You should know that when Mama doesn't hear from you for one week she just can't rest. This time they almost sent you a cable to see if you were alive. Mrs. Shapiro called us up and told us that Lillian intended to come home alone. That was enough to give your mother some food for thought, and she thought of everything under the sun that could have happened to you. Finally after calling Harry Neiman and being convinced that you were O.K. her fears subsided.

Mrs. Shapiro honored us with a visit. She certainly has the gift of gab and she made sure to impress upon us the fact that she was a very charitable soul. However she seems to be quite nice.

Celia, I think you should come home the same time Lillian does. I am going to tell you just how things are. We have had plenty of trouble. I just hate to make you feel bad, but I think you should know that your sister Minnie went off and got married to Al and left the house. She went to live with his people. Mama is broken hearted. She cries her eyes out and looks a sight. That is why I think you should come home sooner. Mama is very lonesome. If you would have been here and seen the scene of Minnie's departure, I am sure you would have felt like putting a knife through the little rat.

Two young men called to get your address. Martin of Newark and Bill.

Without doubt you are aware of the fact that your money in the bank of the U.S. cannot be touched. Your entire capital at present is $52.50 which is in the hands of Mr. Shapiro. Mama is adding one hundred dollars to this $52 and we are sending it out to you. If Mr. Shapiro hasn't sent Lillian's money yet we will send it together.

You really don't deserve to have Papa do this for you. You wouldn't trust your own family with your few dollars. If Papa had your money now, you'd have no worries at all. However, Mama can't be changed. She is pawning her earrings to send you the money so you can travel together with Lillian. Start out as soon as you get the money, Celia, as I think it would be nice for you to be home for the Passover holidays to cheer Mother up a bit.

Everything is O.K. among the rest of the family.

I have a new addition to my family now. Don't misunderstand me, it is only a canary, and he sings beautifully. Joanie also warbles like a canary. She's so adorable. I wish you could hear her dictating to me what to write.

We will not bother to send you the evening gowns. You won't need them if you are coming home.

Love and best regards from all. Regards to Lillian.
Betty

Aug 1948

Papa and Mama Antopolsky

Chapter 12

An ivory cigarette holder

Aaron Antopolsky had traveled alone to America, to get settled in the new place before sending for his family. Two years later Sarah followed, bringing three-year-old Betty. Sarah and Betty passed through the line at Ellis Island while Aaron waited anxiously outside, not certain Sarah would make it through the rigorous inspections. She was a farmer's daughter, short, chunky and energetic, the picture of health, but she suffered from asthma. Early the following year, 1906, Celia was born, and two years after that Irving, and then Minna.

In Poland, Papa Antopolsky had been a salesman, selling windmills to farmers. In America he painted houses. But he still thought like a salesman and knew that the most important thing was to make an impression.

Papa was taller than most people, and cleverer than most, and his eyes were blue and intense under bushy eyebrows. He did nothing in the ordinary way. When he painted a house he decorated the rooms with homemade stencils. He played the violin and the tuba and had played in the Czar's orchestra for his military service. He was meticulous about his clothing and used an ivory cigarette holder.

One year, Papa bought a horse and carriage and paid a man with a barn to keep them, so that on Sundays he could drive his horse around the neighborhood with his family in the carriage, dressed in their best clothes.

Another time, Papa decided he missed the Polish countryside, so he bought a farm in upstate New York and over the protests of his wife and children moved the family to Kingston, New York, to the scrubby patch of land with its leaky farmhouse that was the best he could afford to buy, and there they stayed for an entire year, long enough for him to learn that he wasn't a farmer after all: He was a salesman, and he had sold himself on an idea that made no sense. So they moved back to the house on Liberty Avenue. Celia was eight years old and in the second grade the year they lived on the farm.

On the ground floor of the house on Liberty Avenue was the paint store where neighbors came to buy paint if they wanted to paint their houses themselves, and on the second floor was the living room with a piano in the middle, and bedrooms, and a big kitchen where Mama was always baking bread and cakes to sell and cooking for the family and guests, with her oldest daughter Betty helping and learning how to be a *balabusta*, a good homemaker.

Mama loved to invite relatives and friends to visit and to eat, and on Saturday evenings Papa and the children made music in the living room; in the summer they opened the door at the top of the stairs and neighbors gathered below to listen to the concert. Papa played his violin or his tuba, Betty the accordion, Ike the piano—he could play anything, everyone said, though he had never learned to read music—Celia sang, and Minna danced.

Every Sunday the relatives came to the house (all of them first-generation immigrants) and the men played poker all afternoon while the women talked in the kitchen.

There was a third floor too, and after Betty got married she and her husband, Nat, and later their baby girl Joanie who was the apple of everybody's eye, lived on the third floor and came down for meals and for the Sunday poker game.

—∞—

In the Antopolskys' basement, where Papa mixed his paints and made wine and pickles, a black man called Tea slept on quilts in the corner.

As a child, Celia never thought about the black man in the basement, any more than she thought about the sofa in her parents' living room with its carved wooden feet and tattered upholstery, or the doves her mother kept in a the coop in the back yard, sentimental reminders of the farm in Poland where she had grown up.

Celia, Irving, and Minnie together named the black man.

"He's not really black, not like licorice."

"Not like coffee even."

"More like tea."

So it was decided, and later, Celia didn't remember whether anyone had thought to ask the black man what he thought about it or what his name really was, but then again, Tea never talked at all. Never said a word. In that family where it seemed no one ever stopped talking, Tea stayed down in the basement in the place Mama had fixed for him when he had gotten well enough, with some quilts and later an old mattress someone found. He came up only for his meals or when Mama called him to help move the big wooden chest or sweep the porch or whatever she thought of for him to do. He ate the same food as the family. Mama put a big serving on a plate for him at the top of the stairs and called for him to come get it, and later he brought the empty plate back up from the basement so she could wash it.

Papa had found him in a snowdrift one day in the middle of winter, about to freeze to death, and brought him home and warmed him up, and then he was just there. No one ever knew where he came from. Many times, after a hard day's work, Papa called Tea up from the basement to have a glass of *schnapps* with him, sitting together at the kitchen table, and Tea listened while Papa told him about his day. Then Tea went back into the basement unless Mama had a job for him to do.

Tea lived in the Antopolskys' house for the rest of his life. At the end, my father and my Uncle Irving took him to the hospital and paid his medical and burial expenses, or maybe they only took care of the paperwork so that the government or a charity would pay them.

They didn't tell the rest of the family until many years had passed that Tea had died of syphilis.

Little Celia did very well in school. Papa even said that she didn't need to do chores around the house like the other children. "Celia doesn't have time for that," he said. "She has to study."

How hard Celia worked! How well she did! Winning prize after prize in city-wide essay contests, she taught herself that if she worked hard, if she went over and over her writing until it was as good as she could possibly make it, then it really would be good, better than what anyone else did, good enough to win a prize. Good enough to make people notice. To prove, once again, that she was exceptional.

Chapter 13

To see the World as Beauty
(Letters from Ellis Polonsky to Celia Antopolsky,
November 21, 1930 to November 28, 1930)

Ellis to Celia, November 21, 1930

Marca—

No word from you has come across the seas these ten days and I hope all is well with my comerado. I am not disturbed because I know that our land is an all absorbing one and that my comerado has a weakness for being absorbed.

It is only when one writes frequently that one realizes how dull things are in "golus" [literally, "exile," meaning outside of the land of Palestine]. We must forget the matter of fact things about us and tell a comerado other matters.

We have had two lovely days that have thrown us a handful of gold, probably the last two gold pennies in the pockets of this aging year. And your comerado was moved to stroll up the avenue in the face of all mercenary activities. And of course my comerado came with me and even this dismal and sordid city can look well when bathed in an afternoon's or twilight's golden light. At 36 St we stopped and looked over our shoulders at the clean sweep of the height of steel and stone and we remarked how fine was the silhouette of the church's steeple in brownstone against the new white brick of the Empire State. And my comerado felt the dread of limitation, removed her hat and shook her head and there came forth a flock of golden hair—and I grasped her arm lest I forget my sense of propriety and give in to an urge and pull her hair.

It's good to have a comerado—even if she be in far away lands. So write and tell me that you be.

Ellis

Ellis to Celia, November 24, 1930

Marca Mia—

I too look forward to letters from my comerado and respond acutely to them. If my comerado is happy and contented my pennants flutter in the breeze, if my comerado is lonely and sick at heart—I too am lonely and sick at heart for the distance that separates us makes it impossible to hold her hand and whisper words of comfort to her.

It is good to know that Palestine has become a beautiful part of you. It's good to know that you have responded to its call and it has touched you. But did I not know my comerado's sensitivity, her quickened pulse-beat, her flushed face in the sight of beauty. Oh, it's good to have such a comerado. Even a thought of her stimulates me and to know that she occasionally thinks of her comerado in "golus" pleases me greatly.

What of life about me? It is uninteresting and unimportant. There is little or nothing to report. Nothing to compare to the glorious things about you. Why should I write of it. You have tasted of it and found it lacking and left for finer things. Why should I drag the dross over your gold. I like your gold—do tell me more about it.

Where is my wandering Marca tonight, what new adventure? Wherever she be, whatever she does, go little breeze and whisper to her that I miss her and shall remain her comerado—no matter what happens—

Shalom,
Ellis

P.S. Collected works of Frost just published—we will read it together someday.

ER

Ellis to Celia, November 26, 1930

Marca—

Because I read an essay on Beauty by H. Ellis and because I heard over the radio an inferior rendition of the Sky Blue Waters, and because the first flakes of snow have fallen and because I think of my comerado, I must write in spite of a real press for time, an issue to go to press, in spite of an exam in ten minutes and a multitude of back assignments past due.

Rising sun of the East to you my comerado, silvery moon over the blue Mediterranean and a song from your comerado—I'll be near tonight.

My hand—Marca
Ellis

Ellis to Celia, November 28, 1930

"To see the World as Beauty is the whole End of Living . . . ."
Havelock Ellis, Impressions & Comments—2d Series

Is this not a magnificent credo, my comerado—

Yours for beauty
Ellis

Two years before, while Celia and Lillian were hitchhiking across the United States, Celia had written to Ellis, who was working at a summer camp:

Celia to Ellis, June 30, 1928
Postmark: Las Vegas, N.M.

Full Moon—the 30th of June

Ellis, I would like to have been with you when you were tired, and when you were lonely in the crowd. So many things I could have told you to make you forget—and, oh, you might have told me things. Because I miss you so—tonight badly!—because I would like to give you all the overflow of my experience when you are close by—with my own hands! Each day has stretched amazingly. All those dear things we did together, Ellis, they are irreplaceable. But how royal we would have been where the land is endless—you with seven-league boots and I with a magic carpet—the earth for you, the sky for me, and share and share alike.

. . . One thing only is strong and alike between us. That is the beauty-quest. I may live years in the next few months, you moments, but to each will come the full rewards of his search.

Several men have tried to make love to me. They have fared badly. They do not know of my comerado!

Celia

I hope the moon has sudden meaning for you tonight, as she has for me—I hope she is beautiful for you also—

Chapter 14
Dear boy
*(Correspondence between Harry Neiman and Celia Antopolsky,
December 1930 to February 25, 1931)*

Celia to Harry, December ___ 1930

Why, Harry, dear boy,

I haven't heard from you for a long, long time, or perhaps I haven't written for some time. But the other morning, after it had rained, and the trees were green and shining, I brushed my hand along the wet leaves and touched my lips and then I thought of you vividly, and the boyish shiningness of your eyes, and how you had said once, when I touched your face with rain, that only I would do such a thing. Yes, only I and a million raindrops, that's all.

Don't you want to write to me any more, Harry? Or has sudden prosperity turned you snobbishly away from a poor pilgrim in a strange land? Or has the girl-who-is-most-beautiful caught your love at last, and so fast, that you cannot even have a correspondent five thousand miles away? Dear boy, if you were here for one moment, and I could look at you, I'd know.

If only I didn't live so deeply in the present. If only the past and future mattered more. But they don't—so much—so <u>very</u> much—and now I am utterly captivated by Jerusalem.

I wish I could make you feel it as I do. I want to splash color over your desk and out, out, over the streets you walk through, and about the people you meet and talk to. (Please forgive my unconscious rhymes, if you will not my conscious ones.)

Jerusalem—an old city laid on perhaps the ruins of ten civilizations, an old quarter teeming with Jewish-Arab life, strange smells, embroideries, food stuffs, leather work, metal work, loud barter, squalling babies, hundreds of them, old synagogues, old churches, pious Jews with side-curls and long kaftans, little pious Jews with side-curls and kaftans, fat Christian priests, splendid Arab maidens moving from the hips in grace with heavily-laden trays on their heads, tall aristocratic Bedouins—beautiful specimens of men—with flowing robes and white headdresses, looking each a king in his own right, Shylocks and Arab tradesmen, and lost in it all, an American girl pinching herself to be sure it is she. That's the old city, where David lived and loved.

Then the new quarter—one business street, many narrow lanes winding away from the center of the city, one movie house, British Tommies everywhere, Jewish workers—splendid, strong fellows, speaking Hebrew, singing and working heartily—the mainstay these, and the workers in the agricultural colonies, of the Jewish National Homeland. In the new quarter, also, the great house, built like a fortress, which represents the Keren Kayemeth [Jewish National Fund, founded in 1901 to buy and develop land in Palestine for Jewish settlement]. Many fine residences have been built here also of the white stone so common in Jerusalem.

There is a great peace and quiet in the city, yet an atmosphere of suspicion broods over every thing and people you chat with may be government spies, and no one knows for certain the true state of affairs. Since the White Paper, the national feeling here, sensing the terrific setback implied in the report, has intensified, if possible. There is no question of let-up, though the odds are very great with the British government openly favouring the Arabs. It is only in Palestine, Harry, that the true significance of being a Jew comes to one, here in the scene of the Bible, and one can come to understand better the restlessness of the Jew in other lands. For, essentially, in the wondrously beautiful hills all about Jerusalem there is peace, in thousands of stones lying about, as if asleep, there is peace, and if there were to be war this minute I would still say, "It is impossible, here!"

The full moon in Palestine, Harry, is almost as light as the sun, and a whole world of silver light fills my heart with aching. In the Emek, the valley of Jezreel in which the colonies are, there are still vision, and strength and sincerity. They have so little materially, these people, and yet all the reality and meaning of life seem to be in their songs and in the earth they plow. Life in America becomes meaningless by contrast.

There is no hurry here, no streetcars, no subways. We have a great garden with palms, cypresses and a weeping willow. Pink and white pigeons flutter over the stone courtyard. It is a good life. It is good to live!

Affectionately, dear lad,
Celia

Write to me now! Best remembrance from Lillian. My regards to your office-mate. But I shall come back in the spring perhaps—

Harry to Celia, November 30, 1930

Celia—dear girl,

It seems so long since I heard from you that your last letter came more as a surprise than something expected. Before opening it I said to myself—"this is going to be full of news—she's probably been so very busy doing so many things that they've kept her from writing. But now!" I was not disappointed, only a little sorry that writing to me makes you feel like describing places, and that you yourself are always in the background, merely a writer of geographical letters. Why, Celia, don't you know that much as I enjoy reading about places and people, it's you I want to hear about and read about? Why, your letters end just where they should start—having described the sun—water—landscape—fat sheikhs, mayors' automobiles and what have you—I want to read about

C.A.—but what I do read is "write me everything, always, Celia. Best regards from Lillian."

Miss Nolan, our steno, good, devout little Catholic, came into the room after I read your last letter and caught me letting off some steam—she hasn't spoken to me for days and when she does, shudders and says, "Such swearing! Where were you brought up, Mr. Neiman!" I might have answered, it was all brought on by Jerusalem, although learned on Henry Street.

Now Celia, certainly you do not spend all your time admiring nature.

I expect your next letter to be full of facts—no matter how prosaic—I want facts. What do you do to earn your meals (your money is probably all gone)—have you got some sort of work, what do you do for excitement, what kind of friends do you have, and of course what are the chances of seeing you soon.

NEWS ITEM. There was an election here last Nov. and New Yorkers, having read of every sort of corruption known—and having been shown that it all, and more, was practiced by Tammany Hall, proceeded to reelect its appointees by the greatest plurality ever!!!

We should all be very proud.

Harry

Regards to Lillian.

On December 8, 1930, Harry sent Celia a page torn from the current Saturday Evening Post *with five sonnets by Edna St. Vincent Millay.*

These were just published for the 1st time. I like the 4th best.

Regards. Harry

Pencil draft of a poem written by Celia, after she returned to New York, on the inside back cover of a copy of "Fatal Interview," sonnets by Edna St. Vincent Millay:

Will I ever love as I loved you then,
Dear wild boy of my heart,
With the (singing/raging) mood of it on my lips
And the leaping joy in my eyes,
With the strength of it pulling the earth to our feet
And the song of it lighting the skies?

Will you ever love as you loved me then,
Dear minstrel of my harp,
Pulling the strings with a touch of your lips
Or a gentle nod of your head,
Can it be that the tremulous dream, my love,
Is so soon, ah so very soon, dead?

Celia to Harry, December 21, 1930

Boy, dear,

So, you want facts. Great, wholesome facts. Small, unbeautiful facts. Yes, sir! I hear you, and I'm giving them to you.

First of all, I have left Tel-Aviv, the city of Jews, and have come to live in Jerusalem (note change of address).

Then, I have acquired a teaching position which pays the munificent sum of 8-1/2 pounds or forty-five dollars per <u>month</u>. But that, I'll have you understand, is a living wage, the cost of all things here being very small when compared to the American standard. Can you imagine a whole bread for 7 cents and ten oranges for a nickel?

Lillian has also made some money through teaching and consequently helped the family treasury. Generally, we have far less money than people suspect but, as usual, we really get along very nicely. And we're seeing a whole new country besides.

Lodging: we have a room in a beautiful house with a garden and there's a tree just outside my window (an arrangement that has for long been my secret ambition—a window with a tree) and pink and white pigeons in the courtyard—all for 3-1/2 pounds or $17 per month for both, including furnishings, linen and cleaning service. So you see, we have a bed to sleep in and a roof over our heads when it rains.

Re: my friends: —let it be known to you that new American girls in Palestine are rare novelties and consequently much-sought-after. After a week in Tel-Aviv, we left to escape the rigid social life prescribed by our relatives. But during the first week in Jerusalem, we were invited to seven parties.

The people here are a queer varied lot—a sprinkling of Ph.D.'s, teachers, petty officials, writers, artists, Communists, rabbis and aristocratic labourers. Many men—most bachelors married to their careers—some very fine and clever, others dull as potatoes, some talented, some admirers of talent, and all eager to "make" a new woman on the scene. That's why I've been invited to dine, to wine, to dance, to talk, to walk until I feel that I shall have to return to America to untangle myself emotionally.

But, of course, I'm very much interested in the life, which is full of ease—no hurry, no bustle, no streetcars, no subways. It's almost impossible to make money here as I find to my sorrow. But one needs so little here that a small amount of American money goes a long way. For instance, with $100 I could live nicely until the spring when I plan to return, and I shall probably earn this amount one way or another, Palestine-fashion, i.e. without great hardship.

Meanwhile, I love the land so much that I dread leaving the eternal spring here, the blue skies and warm sun, for bleak, jobless America. Do you see, dear lad? Oh, I do wish you could come here. Please believe that I think of you again and again, and sometimes I want you, when the night is filled with moonlight and longing. And I don't write because I'm so absorbed in it all.

Lillian wants to return with the Mauretania in March. I may go back with her then especially if we gather enough money, somehow, to make a flying trip through Europe on the way back.

But just now, I am living in the present with only letters to remind me of the past. New York seems terribly remote, but it's good to think someone cares whether we are getting along well or not, you dear far-sighted one, and really wants to know the facts!

It's past one now. Good night, my lawyer, my dear friend, my would-be manager—yes, I think I'll let you kiss me good-night this time. No, only once—

Celia

Harry to Celia, December 30, 1930

Dear Celia,

I did not mean for it to appear that I refuse to write out of turn; that before I write there must have been an answer to my previous letter. But rather, I did not write because it seemed to me that both of us really had nothing to say and so, to me, the wisest course appeared to let things slide awhile until there was more to justify doing so than custom.

I've discovered, Celia dear, that with me, out of sight is, almost, out of mind. You can realize, then, with what eagerness I receive your letters, for honestly, you are one of the things I do not want to, nor can afford to forget; and while I must admire the easy beautiful flow of words and the realistic pictures you draw, I can't shake the feeling that only the externals are for me, that the <u>you</u> deep down that thinks and feels is withheld, while the seeing you reports to me in almost essay style what is seen. Do you know that your letters could be sent to others almost as duplicate originals and they would not appear misdirected? In other words, they are too impersonal—classically cold—all this sounds sort of cranky and oldish—but you will understand.

(Why can't the stuff you publish be as well-written?)

You ask, "have you fallen in love with the beautiful girl and has prosperity snobbishly turned you away"? I might say that I have seen as much of the beautiful girl as I have of prosperity and so I am still fancy free. Need I say more? (Out of sight, out of mind.) Alas!

You have learned, I guess, of the terrible state of affairs in New York and elsewhere in the United States. Unemployment is increasing daily and bread lines include people who only yesterday were comfortably well-fixed. It is a common sight to see men and women with baskets of apples—4 or 5 on a corner—selling them at 5 cents apiece—people, for the most part, who look not at all like peddlers.

From the above you will gather that I am making lots of money. The sad truth is that I am not, though with $124.54 in the bank (you remember I started with much less) I shouldn't complain. What with a $110.—rent bill at home and household expenses and nobody contributing I shouldn't complain if I only manage to make ends meet.

There are many wonderful moving pictures and shows on display at this time and in spite of all the depression people pay $2.20 to see and hear Lawrence Tibbett and Grace Moore in "New Moon," Ronald Colman in "The Devil to Pay," Ina Claire and Fredric March (which by the way is worth coming from Palestine to see) in "The Royal Family of Broadway" (the Barrymores of course), Fritz Lieber in his Shakespearian repertoire and a host of other interesting shows with all the old favorites very much in evidence.

Hope you are happy dear girl and may happiness be yours in the new year and always. Regards to Lil.

Harry

Harry to Celia, January 14, 1931

Dear Celia,

Received your letter chock-full of facts and thanks very much for it. Now I know that you are most anxious to go home and I, for one, won't be surprised to see you here even before March. Whether you like to

Outings

hear so or not I do think that you miss the hustle and bustle of life in NY, the noisy street cars, heavy traffic, subways, crowds, etc., in fact you miss them so much that you give yourself away by repeating over and over, "life is so full of ease here, etc., etc." Come ahead, I'm waiting.

It was good to hear how nicely you've caught on in Palestine, of your numerous friends (don't let them move you—don't let anyone move you before I do) and the truly fine job you've landed. There's no denying, you do have a way about you. There's many a would be school teacher here in NY who has lost her job at Macy's (they "laid-off" 2600 after Christmas) and makes less than $45 a month—and some lawyers, too. Is that an indictment? Alas!

The low cost of living in Palestine intrigues me. Is it really true, and Celia, are American fellows as much of a novelty and as much sought after as American girls? If so, instead of going to some swell Jewish place in upstate New York for 2 weeks, I could go to Palestine for 3 months—that is, if I could fly.

This letter is being written at 11:30 p.m. at my office after having been a good Samaritan and introduced a love-lorn adolescent young lawyer to a lady of ill fame with whom he has gone away to find for himself happiness in this vale of tears and small fees. I predict a sadder and wiser and poorer man tomorrow morning.

Having satisfied a friend, resisted temptation, saved my money and written my letter (such as it is), there is nothing left for me to do but have some coffee at the Automat (I know you'd like to see one again) and go home.

Good night, darling. Thanks for the kiss, but you never used to be so stingy.

Harry

Regards to Lillian.

Harry to Celia, February 7, 1931

Dear Celia,

"We will be talking it over in the spring, perhaps," you say. What can I say but come ahead, quick, for I miss you, dear, and all you stand for, believe me. I miss your generous smile, your funny, fuzzy, blond mop of hair that always made me think, "could anyone but Celia keep it in order and actually make it look an asset to one's appearance?" And then, too, no one can say "hello Harry" and make the words sound just how you do.

When I received your card I would have liked to answer immediately but was in the midst of preparation of a case for trial and it (the case) has kept me busy since. Many nights at 11 p.m. and at 12 midnight I would be at the office working at it, and finally last Friday it came on for trial before a judge and jury and I recovered a judgment for $2,180—the largest so far for me—and what is more imp't my compensation was to be ¼ of all sums recovered. Was I happy?! But before leaving me at the door the attorney on the other side said, "Say, do you know, I'm going to file a petition in bankruptcy for these people?" I almost fainted. Nor have I gotten over it yet. I had neglected many little matters for this one and looked forward to and banked upon making enough out of this case to <u>carry</u> me for a while. Alas the judge granted 5 days stay of execution (Lillian will explain what that means) and it may well be that I'm being <u>kidded</u> for the purposes of effecting a settlement of my judgment; I'll know next week for sure.

[Crossed out: Does it make any difference if I say that it would please me to hear from you more often?] Please disregard. I'm selfish.

Best wishes—remember me to Lillian.

Harry to Celia, February 14, 1931

Dear,

Your letter came in time for me to assure your family that their dutiful daughter, who had not written to them for over a month, was well, apparently happy, and intended to come home next April or earlier. I was ashamed for you, sweet, and ventured the suggestion that your mail had miscarried—send four or five letters off right away, ungrateful, thoughtless, child.

It makes me unhappy to cause you disappointment but the truth is that my mustache is no more, having been done away with just when it was assuming brush-like proportions, because my public clamored for the restoration of the "real American type," claiming that I had gone Communistic. When you return I may retire from public life and raise a new one; one which instead of wiggling good-naturedly would "bristle" fiercely. That would please you wouldn't it? But where I shall acquire a chin that can settle back "rock-like" I do not know. One thing is quite clear, what with the necessity of acquiring a bristling moustache, a rock-like chin and a full grown beard between now and April (the approx time of your expected return) much work must be done in a very short time. But they do say Ed. Pinaud's Tonic can do wonderful things.

How clever, really, of you to so completely understand the sort of letter that would please me, and how nice of you to be so agreeable and send one to my order. It did suit my vanity very much, for in it I counted two (2) "dears" and one or two phrases turned to my liking. What caused me to laugh, however, was that I missed the scenery in the letter. I _am_ being hard to please, N'est-ce pas?

I remember that day in the woods when I saw Celia as she is: How could I forget? The eager, wide eyed, child-like look in your face in the presence of beauty brought to me Edna St. V. Millay's line, "Ah world I cannot hold you close enough." That was how you looked, and for me that look meant only, "I must see more of this girl." And when you leaned forward and, oh so tenderly, cupped some wild flower in the palm of your hand excitedly calling me to admire its beauty, I thought, "I hope we can become friends." We did, and are now, I think. And, of course, we'll see each other when you get back—and you're going to get a few millions of words off your chest—and I'm going to get rid of countless kisses, two for every word you say.

It is 3 o'clock in the morning. The last six hours have been spent with a girl who is truly beautiful. I feel unsatisfied; something is missing. That something I've tried to describe in the preceding paragraph; that something you have, dear Celia, and so, just now, I am fancy free. Did you say April?

Love,
Harry

Harry

Harry to Celia, February 25, 1931

Sweet—

Real news this time!

On Washington's Birthday, after taking a walk from my house in the Bronx across town to the river, and then along it to 42 St and the famous Caruso restaurant, and then to the library, resolved to do some honest to goodness beneficial reading and actually ran into that very interesting fellow, Lillian's brother Harold, who, upon seeing me, lost no time in popping this question, "Are you and Celia keeping company? There's such a rumor going about!?"

Then and there I showed my greatness. It would have been easy to answer à la Tammany Hall, "I refuse to answer on the grounds that it might incriminate me," or to hide behind the smart aleck remark, "how can I be keeping company with someone more than 5000 miles away," or again, to quibble and say "do you mean in the sense of seeing something of each other, spending time together? Or do you mean going about with intent to marry?" and so I said, "Ceil and I are very good friends I hope and feel, just that and nothing more." Was I not right? That's how you'd have answered.

Harold thinks you will be home in a few weeks. I hope he's right.

Harry

Chapter 15

Shout through the streets of Zion

(Letters from Ellis Polonsky to Celia Antopolsky,
December 17, 1930 to February 26, 1931)

Ellis to Celia, December 17, 1930

Marca,

It seems a long time since I've last had a chat with you and I've felt as if I had been missing something. The letter which I last answered left me in such an indecisive mood as to our future plan of procedure that I feared to continue our correspondence until you cleared up some matters. But you are my comerado, until you say differently and then that might affect our behavior not our correspondence. Recently there appeared a very interesting story in the paper of the imminent publication of the beautiful and affectionate correspondence between the beautiful actress Terry and George Bernard Shaw. The correspondence was most affectionate and intimate and their letters most beautiful. By this means they built up a delicately wrought friendship. Now the strangeness of this was that only once in their lives had they met and that was for a short business talk. This correspondence indicated a sincere love for each other and both of them kept from meeting each other for fear of disappointment. At one time she lived but a few blocks from him and used unusual restraint in keeping from running to him. While reading the article there kept running in my mind a line that somehow expressed my sentiments: "I am half-sick of shadows, said the lady of Shalott."

And so they lived and loved and she died without pressing the hand of her lover. The vicarious love was beautiful but lacked a certain courage— Now what has this to do with us—I don't know except if we are to remain physically apart I should still cherish our communion of a wish expressed, a hope, a thought.

Einstein came to America for Chanukah and he was accepted by America as no king has ever been. I was thrilled, even callous I, was thrilled. First, when he was received by Walker and introduced by Nicholas Murray Butler who labeled him the "Monarch of the Mind," the band played "Wacht Am Rhine" [a German patriotic anthem] and then just as proudly it blasted forth "Hatikvah." A gesture from Walker, but recognition that this man, greatest of the minds, accepts his people and he is accepted as one of them.

The next night all of New York Zionism gathered in Madison Square Garden to commemorate Chanukah. 14,000 Jews packed the huge decorated hall to celebrate the Maccabean victory. Word passed around that Einstein refusing most other invitations had consented to join the celebration. How proud they all were of this fellow Jew.

At eleven o'clock, there appeared a long line of policemen, behind whom there came a half frightened man, smiling to keep courage, holding on to his more aggressive wife. As Einstein stepped to the stage, the audience, touched by his presence, raised their heads and sang from the depths of their hearts, Hatikvah. For the moment there was no Golus, for the moment we were home, all of us. I have heard Hatikvah sung in the face of adversity, I heard Hatikvah sung in the midst of speaking demagogues, but never was there more spirit and pathos than there was in the song of greeting to one of its faithful sons. There were tears in his eyes and in the eyes of those watching him as they refused to stifle their emotion and sang a second time Hatikvah. Had Passfield, Chancellor or MacDonald heard that, they would have known how dear to the hearts of this people Palestine is.

The man himself has a most boyish face under a crop of white hair—wind blown. More than his boyish face is his boyish attitude. It was as if this little boy had been kept in seclusion all his life and then brought to Coney Island. Or it reminded me of my walking into the cathedral, half frightened, holding the hand of my more experienced comerado. [This would be midnight Mass on Christmas Eve at St. Patrick's Cathedral; young Jews liked to go for the spectacle.] So to him, his wife was his more experienced social guide who held his hand and shielded him against a super-social sharp-edged society.

He sat on the stage and stared about him, noticing the packed galleries and the solid mass of humanity in front of him, and he was visibly impressed. He probably didn't know that his every motion was being watched closely. He partly rose from his chair and swung his arm in a semi-circle pointing out to his wife the crowds in the gallery. He was absolutely excited as he saw so many thousands of Jews packed into the Garden. His love for music was evident, as he raised his hand instinctively to quiet the crowd as a singer was rendering an aria from "Tosca." He jumped up to shake the hand of Yossele Rosenblatt when he finished singing L'Zion. On occasion after occasion his wife would call his attention to something or someone that society demands of a guest.

I stared at him and wondered that this man with a minor social intelligence should have such a major and almost infinite grasp of universal formulae. It was all a lovely occasion and we sang until the wee hours of the morning. Hora and hora, song and song, this was a prayer, this was a hope.

Ussisshkin remarked to Edna Sue, who is his secretary now, that he remembered you with the "Mischugener hur" [crazy hair].

I'd send you a snowflake if I didn't know your half-fear of cold.

Feb. 17—Exam for School Psychologist.

Thanks for the flower and [illegible]—oh for a bivouac among the pines.

Your comerado,

Ellis

Ellis to Celia, December 29, 1930

To a carefree flower in the sun—that is Marca—

It is so good to hear from you and to know that you are happy and at ease. Nothing makes me so radiant as to know that you are free of care and that untroubled you can absorb the beauty around you. Marca, how I love you when you're smiling and happy and how broken I am when I see you unhappy and depressed. Know this Marca, when I have made you unhappy, I have also suffered much and as long as your head drooped with sadness there was a depressing load upon my heart. And as soon as your head was raised and the sun dried your tears and your hair glistened— I was relieved and I knew that it was Marca.

It is all so lovely, the things you write of Jerusalem. It is little wonder that New York is a large, ugly reality to you in Jerusalem. And now too, I am a bit carefree for Wednesday I am off to the woods for a few days. I shall have trees, and hills and only my comerado shall be lacking. I'm going to the Suffern Bear Mt. trail—the spot we fell exhausted upon and looked for our breeze to cool us on that stifling hot day. If I persist, I will cover the bivouacs of some two years ago where we spent a glorious two days, one being wet but not dampened. And I shall mark the spots that my comerado will love and someday, if she returns, we shall go to the woods and I shall show my comerado what I have saved and prepared for her.

How I should like to swing down the road with my comerado at my side. It is on the road I miss her most.

Soon there shall be no snow. Soon dogwood shall blaze across the landscape, soon the trails shall burst with greenness and the icy ground will melt into a softness under foot. Birds will come with spring and I must come too.

When I miss you most and the hurt becomes more poignant I shall go in search of a lilac tree—two stories high—I swear it. I shall find you in the woods or not at all.

Little do we live here except in the future; little do we have here except in hopes.

Oh I know of your pressing social activities, I know of your many engagements and your absorbing companionships and I forgive and understand your delays in writing.

You wrong me in your remark of my lack of appreciation of H.N. I've never said anything about him which has not been said in praise, I've never uttered a word of adverse criticism. I've told you that I thought he was fine looking, clean cut and pleasing.

Comerado, I am

Ellis

Poem by Celia Antopolsky, published in *The Poet and the Critic*, September, 1930:

I Did Not See the Lilac Tree

I am awake to some sweet memory of you
That leans between the walls across the room,
And pours into the dark the fragrance of
A shadow-fingered lilac tree in bloom.

You told me once with all endearment you could bring,
The somewhere in the springtime there would be,
A full two stories high, (I dared not doubt),
The magic of a budding lilac tree.

Night has come slowly, with the growing tint
Of lilacs when the light has left their face,
And I have thought of green and grassy peace
That we shall stir when you find me the place.

Come, come quickly, boy-mine, let me see,
Before the year turns to itself and dies,
Beauty born eternal out of love,
Come, let me see with my own eyes.

Ellis to Celia, January 6, 1931

Marca Mia—

I am always writing to you—when I am not writing actually, I am looking forward to the moment when I can and thinking of all the things I would like to shout across to you or perhaps some of the things I would whisper.

Listen Marca—there was a fairy queen with eyes that were soft for crying, a mouth that was poised for smiling and hair that scattered gold with its shaking. But most beautiful was her soul and what the eyes saw the soul felt deeply. Beauty touched her as a penetrating lance that reached to the strings of her soul to make music and her whole body trembled with the rhythm of the music.

She was destined to live in a dark and cold city in which she hungrily searched for warmth and beauty. Her soul suffered for the lack of music. In her search she met a prosaic comerado who upon closer acquaintance gave forth almost inaudibly a strain of low and simple music. And the princess was happy and the comerado was glad.

Hand in hand they scoured the scene in search of music and they found the beauty in strange places. When the gold was lacking they found it in themselves. They built walls between themselves and the cold, ugly realities—and what was beyond the wall—they didn't care at all, at all.

The spirit of the princess was like a gentle zephyr she and her comerado had learned to love and her feet were as light as the golden fringes of spring. The spirit of her comerado was like the same zephyr but his feet were like the roots of trees.

One day there came to the ears of the princess the story of a land of blue and gold, of sunny hill and fragrant field and her soul longed for the land of sunshine. Knowing her spirit and his roots, her comerado urged her go; knowing his soul, she bade him come. But strain as he would the roots budged not.

With the spirit of the zephyr and the feet of golden fringes she sped to her dreamland and was happy except when she longed for her comerado in the city of dross.

Days grew cold for the comerado rooted in the soil and the warmth came only from the letters of his princess in the land of gold and blue.

A day came when the spirit of the princess could not fly for the weight of trouble that rested on it. And all the elements of the beauty of the land which had come to love the princess were sorry. A crocus caught itself in the sandal of the princess and as she kneeled to free the entangled bit of beauty (because she was tender with flowers), she lifted the face of the flower towards her face when she heard the flower say,

"Dear princess, your spirit is heavy with care. Why do you not fly today," and the eyes that were soft for crying dropped a tear that was as sweet as the dewdrop on the face of the crocus. She told the crocus of the rooted comerado who was held in a cold city whose spirit too longed for warmth of gold and blue. And lo and behold the crocus lifted his face and called to a song bird and the song bird sang to a zephyr and the zephyr scooped a handful of gold and carried it over land and seas to the city of her comerado and his soul flew to great heights and there was music in his heart.

And the princess was happy. I will write soon.

Ellis

Ellis to Celia, January 9, 1931

Just because it's a fine day tinted by the glow of Erev Shabbos and filled with beautiful thoughts of you—on Fridays, I have to stay and write my comerado. And say

Shabbat shalom [Have a good Sabbath; written in Hebrew letters]

I am on the verge of being engulfed in a swirl of work and before I am overcome, I must be able to say a few words to you in the ease with which I have always spoken to you.

Feb. 17 is the date of the exam for school psychologist and I intend to take a chance at it, if they let me.

Then that damn thesis—yes the same one. Funny, but even without the pleasant distraction of you, I have done nothing on it—and since my CAREER depends on the completion of the work before May, I shall be forced to work hard and fast. Pity me, pity me your comerado who will be broken under the chains of servitude.

Already the cold is showing signs of going with the coming of a few golden days now and then. And every now and then comes a day that speaks the language of Palestine and I think so fondly of a comerado.

Tyl is married! And there goes one of my best chances. Yisgodal. V'yis kodosh [the first words of the Kaddish, the mourners' prayer]. Married last week in order to amuse her brother who had come in for a vacation.

I spent a few days in the woods that was blanketed with untrammeled snow and that was brightened with the fullness of a brilliant moon—and the sky has so many stars—I was quiet and sad—for then I wanted to shout for my comerado.

It is time for candles. Goodnight, my Marca

Ellis

Ellis to Celia, January 20, 1931

Marca—so you are my comerado—and you do miss me.

The roots are too deep to be plucked out from our hearts and allowed to shrivel. They are too tightly riveted to the sensitive strings that vibrate with beauty. I was glad to hear that my letters were friends that bring cheer rather than words that torture you.

Let all your uneasiness disappear and accept me with these few thoughts.

I will remain your devoted comerado in the face of anything. I shall be your comerado not only because you need a comerado but because I too need you as a comerado. No other tie shall be strong or deep enough to keep me from you, my Marca. Nothing you do or no tie you have shall drive me from you, unless I know that you desire it in your sane moments (and they are few).

So this is the story of one comerado as he stretches out his hand to another comerado. This is the call of an earnest heart to a receptive soul and Spring around the corner.

It is strange Marca, that I feel so deep an almost possessive interest in you. An interest that understands and delights in you. No matter what you had said, I would have gone on feeling that at least part of you belongs to me. You could fume and frown and shake your troublesome locks, denying that you care at all for me and I would wink and smile and say to myself, "She does." And that isn't conceit.

Days are getting more goldenlike and gentle and bleak cold is coming less frequently—and I am missing my comerado more and more poignantly (poiñantly).

But next to having her near is to know that she is happy and still misses me some—

Friends may come and friends may go—but comrades go on forever—

Your comerado,
Ellis

Ellis to Celia, January 28, 1931

Marca Mia,

If I were to take your emotional outburst seriously—something I <u>rarely</u> do, I would be driven to distraction. It would be like the heartless plucking of a daisy, "she loves me," "she loves me not."

"I need you," "I've learned to be independent." "Maybe you will fall in love with me again," "I am glad I have learned to be independent." But I know you Marca, I can see your surface indifference covering that explosive tearful love of me and I know, were I near, I could touch it off and all your resisting barriers would be washed away in the flood of tears.

I am coming home to Palestine! Seriously I have started saving for the great occasion. I have tentatively signed up for a camp job in order to raise more money and I shall add it all up to make enough to go in September. This time I really mean it and feel it and the thought of it makes me happy.

The resolve came over me at once and with accumulating enthusiasm I have taken steps to carry it out. School will be no more—and ties will be severed and I shall go to a land that has enchanted me. Your letters probably did a great deal to make me resolve this plan.

Maybe Marca will await my coming and take her comerado in hand (like she did one day in a strange cathedral) and show me the land.

How long I shall stay I do not know—but go I will for go I must.

Our birthday [shared, February 12] is coming nearer and my comerado so far away. I shall write more soon.

Shout through the streets of Zion that a lover cometh (as if anybody would be interested).

Love,
Ellis

Ellis to Celia, January 29, 1931

Marca—

[Enclosure: list of names and addresses of teenagers seeking Palestinian pen-pals.]

The eagerness to write to their brothers and sisters in Palestine goes on unabated—even in Cincinnati. These children are anxious to correspond and notice the sex desired [almost all, boys and girls, want to correspond with a boy]. Oh that insidious sex—but who am I to interfere with the urges. And do you notice the neglect of the "Girls."

But there is one girl I intend to write to in Palestine. I shall hope to receive many letters from a certain Marca, alias Celia Antopolsky.

Excuse me. This was meant to be a business letter. Ahem—please take care of the requests.

Yr businesslike comerado,
Ellis

P.S. Step 1 on the Palestine trip—I made that deposit in the bank.

Ellis to Celia, February 3, 1931—Return address, his parents' apartment in The Bronx. Paper folded around the letter bears the message: "To keep inquisitive eyes from the message to my Comerado"

Marca—

Remember the day we sat together and acted and read the "Affairs of Anatol." Remember the ebullient second Act, which is the parting scene between Anatol and one of his ladies. They had agreed that when either party would desire to break off the relationship, they would frankly announce their intention and the other would simply and sympathetically accept "the end of a love or a season." Anatol has decided to end the romance and invites his friend Max along to give him courage and to stand by the outburst of tears of the jilted damsel. But lo and behold the damsel beats Anatol to it and announces her intention to terminate the affair which completely demoralizes Anatol's pride and the scene ends in a frenzy of accusations.

Well, anyhow, I saw the opening of that delightful play with Joseph Schildkraut and Miriam Hopkins set in charming Vienna, interwoven with the lilting waltzes of Strauss. It was a rare treat even though J.S.'s form was a bit stiff. You would have loved it—you with your affairs would have seen the consequences and conceits behind them.

During the last two weeks I have managed to read a splendid sociological treatise called "Marriage and Morals" by Bertrand Russell. It is the new and wholesome thought behind the moth eaten covering of what might be a beautiful and inspiring social relationship. He speaks frankly and plainly and corroborates with me on most of my theories.

Either Feb. or March I shall take an apartment for myself in the Village or downtown NY. You must come over.

This letter is a very sober and newsy one, I suppose in order to make up for that most affectionate and sentimental epistle of two days ago.

Nevertheless I do want to remain one of the major "affairs of Celia" and the only "affair of Marca."

Comerado,

Ellis

From Bertrand Russell, "Marriage & Morals":

". . .The proper course, if the biological function of marriage were adequately recognized, would be to say that no marriage should be legally binding until the wife's first pregnancy. . . . This view depends, at least in part, upon that separation between procreation and mere sex which has been brought about by contraceptives."

Ellis to Celia, February 4, 1931 (paper folded around letter)

Marca, I miss you

Soon it will be our birthday and we shall be so far apart that it will take a stretching of a comerado's hand to reach a comerado far away.

How I would love to have you here so we could spend one glorious day together. But we shall have our celebration yet—even if it be delayed some months.

If you are in Palestine when I arrive in October, you will take me by the hand and lead me about the cities and the colonies and we shall be so happy, even at this belated date—

Or if you postpone your visit to the continent until the end of September, I shall go there and I (not Santos or whatever his name is) will meet you in front of the Opera—and we shall stroll strange streets and stop at open cafes for a drink and resume our journey thru the Louvre, Versailles, Bois Boulogne? And we shall celebrate our birthday 7 months late in strange places and we shall be happy, together.

Or if the urge of the States or them what's in it becomes too great and you decide to return, it shall be a happy and cheerful Spring—and I shall turn my eyes away from the East for a moment to welcome my comerado— and there will be the greenness of the woods and the singing of birds that call for my comerado and me. And we shall go alone into the woods and we shall climb to a windswept hill and in our bivouac a breeze shall move my comerado and we shall tell each other tales and tales—and we shall be happy.

Choose my Marca—will you have your comerado in the quaint streets of Paris, away and alone with only a comerado? At home in the interrupted sunlight of a golden land in the east—or a holiday in the rush of a not very ugly city in the spring?

Only this I know. That in September, I leave America and for what part I shall aim will depend a great deal on what my comerado will do. It may be that I shall take the Fabre Line direct to Zion or a European line to Europe.

I understand that Meyer Miller teaches at the same place you do? What's the chance of getting a good job teaching, or anything else. You know my B.S. is in education and I majored in English—Why not sign me up at your school for next fall.

Marca, mia, write and tell me many things. Don't you have a real address beside Poste Restante—or are you keeping your private life a secret from me?

Birthday greetings
Your own comerado
Ellis

I have already saved $75 in a week's activity. I expect to sign up for a camp job at $350.

Ellis to Celia, February 11, 1931 (paper folded around letter)

Marca comerado—

Tomorrow is a very uneventful birthday with you thousands of miles away. It is strange how little there is now in birthdays without you near. And yet a few years ago I could celebrate unrestrained a birthday—all of this and most other pastimes are engulfed in the great desire and the certain plans for my trip in September. There is no rumoring or questioning, no conditions or probabilities; it is certain that I go to Palestine, if God spares me and there are no unforeseen tragedies.

It is strange how impatient I have become and how hours and days seem to stretch in an over-fullness. How I guard each step towards the trip and how I brush aside any possible obstacle to it, how thrifty I have become because of it and how much foresight I manifest in planning it, all of it would surprise you. It is still stranger that I have a constant dread that something may happen to keep me from it. I wear rubbers more often and button my coat in order to prevent anything seriously affecting me. So you see I do want to go to Palestine and I am almost in the position of my character in "If I forget thee O'Jerusalem" [a story, apparently written by Ellis] who stands ready to leave for Zion and questions whether he goes because of his love for Zion or his love for Luba who is also going. This I know that for 2000 years I have missed Zion and its new beauty and beauty is synonymous with Marca—and together it will be "Gan Eden" [the Garden of Eden].

Shall I go through the continent or direct to Palestine? If you can meet me in France or Germany I will go there, if you will meet me at Jaffa, I will go there. It would be fun to be able to spend a month or so in the quaint city of Paris, finding a Madison Street, running through Rue This and Rue That. Exploring its Latin Quarter, walking on its boulevards, drinking at the cafés, steering clear of the Americans—just the two of us like "Babes in the Woods"—from there across the continent to the Mediterranean to Palestine—if we have enough money. If plans work out as I expect I should have $700 in all.

So you see I've accepted the challenge of your last letter and I am coming to see you.

Marks is elated at Lillian's plan to return and he is getting all excited about possibilities. I have positively ordered that all gifts to me be for practical purposes so that they can be of use on my trip. Now do you see how practical I have become. One gift nevertheless was a beautiful volume called the "Last Days of Shylock" by Ludwig Lewisohn. It is well written and finely illustrated by Syzk.

I am coming home—will my comerado wait—

Ellis

Ellis to Celia February 24, 1931

Past the $100 mark

Marca—

Nothing of importance exists here for me, all my efforts and interests are in the direction of Palestine—and everything points to my going. Even my family has accepted my going and show a curiosity in the details. I have become thrifty, nay miserly—most of my money goes to the bank, this week I shall have $150. I tremble at the thought of something going wrong and there is one thing that bothers me. My camp job has been hard hit because of the horrible times and my earlier disinterest. Now that I want money from camp, most of the jobs have been taken and I find only offers of $250. And this year because I want money so badly—well $250 all at once is better than $30 or $40 in the city. How much will I need and can you get me a job as head of English Department. You know I am a graduate of School of Ed and English major. Maybe you'll tell B_____ of my coming.

I do so hope you will stick to your earlier threats and stay in Palestine. If we could spend a year together uninterruptedly it would be a great and beautiful experience. I have been and am very impatient to hear your reaction which I expect in a week.

Write me and tell me you'll be there when I come—I leave early in Sept—no matter what happens.

Love
Ellis

Ellis to Celia, February 26, 1931

Feb. 26—
Acct $150

My Captive Maiden—

Your lovely book of prints thrilled me and sharpened the already keen edge of my desire. How some of your thoughts amuse me in the newer light of my coming adventure.

Nary a letter comes that does not call forth the lovely sentiment that "how happy I would be if you were here" or "if you were here I should probably never want to return." And I smile as these letters keep piling up and I say "I've called her bet, we will see if her sentiment are sincere."

So annoying are letters that are a month stale. I do love all your letters but I wanted so to have the last letter shriek forth "Ellis, I will wait, I am happy you are coming home." But having left you before my news reached you, it was miserably mute, mute was my captive maiden.

How I wish I could take seriously "my little butterfly" who threatens to move on and light on other spheres and who warns me not to place my trust in distant places. But I'll come near and I shall be unrestricted to woo her and perhaps she will stay with me a while.

It is no surprise that Lilly is returning as it is no surprise that you are remaining. One has to feel deeply to stay long in Palestine.

I should like to stay on in Palestine a long time. I should like to do something useful there. I do not want to be a tourist, I want to be a part of its soul, no its body, its working and brawny body.

Perhaps you can arrange for me to fill some sort of position, the head of an English Dept. or a bank, or the Executive. I would like to know what it would be like to work side by side with you and be free to devote all my time to you.

I know that you are saying "But I shall have other friends and I do not want to devote all my time to you." And I am answering "Your comrade brings you no ties, he brings you freedom." I shall know when my comerado wants me.

I shall probably leave on S.S. Alesia in early Sept. or perhaps even earlier on a trans European trip. The bank account grows and so does my desire—and comerado it is true I come even if it be with a tiny surplus of $.

Because I want my comerado and I want my land.

I hereby authorize you to sign me up for any job starting the middle of Oct. on the condition it isn't past walking distance from you. How long I shall stay depends upon you and the land and you.

I shall come armed with a B.S. in Education—English major and M.A. in Psychology—qualified School Psychologist and a friend of a teacher of English in Jerusalem.

And you, Marca Pola, tell me what does a traveler wear, take, eat? What shall I bring, send and leave behind? How shall I come—and where will you meet me?

Feb. is gone, March is here.

I am coming Marca

Love

Ellis

Chapter 16
Ellis, sex and Nietzsche
(Excerpts from Celia Antopolsky's journal,
November 28, 1928 to May 25, 1929)

November 28, 1928:

Marca I am for ["Ellis" is heavily crossed out and replaced by "singing"],
Celia for all the world, but Sevia is alone. She will always be alone in her
whiteness, that best segment of me. No, not a segment, for she is a unity
or more than unity. When I see Sevia Antopolska in dark, inscrutable
print, I am amazed at my distance from this lovely molder of dream
stuff. Never have I so clearly seen her in outline, though I have felt the
strong beating of her wings from the darkness within me.

"You must have chaos in you,
If you would give birth to a dancing star." [Quotation from Nietzsche].

Nietzsche has spoken of the superman. In me is the super-woman if
sensitivity and strength of vision and potentiality for passion are to be the
triple gauge. But the superb technical power and spiritual resistance that
will hurl such a woman to a mountain-top are merely seeds now that may
shrivel to nonentity in an atmosphere of insignificance.

What shall I do with the man who is at my lips, my throat, my breast?
What shall I do if his kiss like a double-edged sword haggles the harp of
my strength until the strings of energy are loose and spiritless? He tells
me it is ecstasy to be lost before a man's sweeping passion. I say it is that
succumbing which undermines the genius of women in the ultimate crisis

of man vs. woman. Could we gain the experience without loss of strength we would retain our greatness. It is because, by precedent, or convention, or innate desire, we wish ardently to merge ourselves into man that for the greatest woman there has always been necessary a greater man.

I shall write a book of the super-woman. It shall be the voice of the machine that is modern woman. It shall also be the wireless voice of woman into the future. How simple it will be to make divisions—
Seed—small girl—wakening girl—tree-growing girl—budding girl—first woman—beautiful woman—full, ripe woman—branching woman—fruit-bearing woman—autumn woman—woman of winter—Death, add the eternal spring woman—

Now I can carry it only to first woman for I am still looking at these things with wondering eyes and am greatly amazed and deeply hurt.

But oh, now I am happy in the silence and loneliness of the day for I have seen a vision of what is to come to pass, and I shall drive the horses to the sun, and I shall drink with them of the light, and I shall be hurled back to earth—that I may rise again.

There is only one more entry in the journal:

May 25, 1929

In the face of a man's desire, though the man be her dearest friend, a woman is ultimately, basically, alone.

Chapter 17

Are you too moulding dream hills?

(Letters from Ellis Polonsky to Celia Antopolsky,
March 3, 1931 to April 1931)

Ellis to Celia, fragment, undated [March 3, 1931?]

Now, I with my modest bank account have become a financier: Yesterday, Marks asked for a loan of $50 to send to Palestine for Lillian. Today I made the only withdrawal on my account to help a friend in need. $200 has become $150 but it will soon be back.

Ellis to Celia, March 9, 1931

Marca Mia—

It is good that you will wait and the moons shall move lazily but they shall move. Now, already one has gone and I shall come in less time than you can answer five letters of mine. Lost in the East with Marca—and even this stolid comerado shall travel post haste across half the world and maybe he shall earn the title of a fitting companion for Marca.

Know, Marca, that the greatness of my desire has brushed everything aside. The longing for you and the land has driven all other longings before it. That days and months drag in a most piteous pace and that I have become miserly in my financial maneuvering. My most enjoyable trips are to the bank and my most enjoyable dreams are those of Sept. and Oct. and Nov. etc. ad infinitum. And that I come with no set plan and that there is no limit to the time I will have.

Marca your comerado is impatient—

Love,

Ellis

Ellis to Celia, March 10, 1931, enclosing playbill from the New Amsterdam Theatre

Marca, my playmate—

I think there is nothing I want to do more and nothing I need more than to play with you.

Do you remember in the blessed Madison Colony [the Apartment], how I started downstairs to go to school and work and how I stopped in to say "good morning" and how I stopped to read with you, the Golden Apple—you and I on the floor—that was playing. Do you remember how we came home late one night clutching pipes for "blowing bubbles" and wax for modeling—that was play.

And today I am all for "fairys and bubbles" and I miss my comerado so—for, what's a comerado for if not for playing—and you will be my fairy princess won't you—in a strange but beautiful land.

And here is why I am so whimsy—last night I was taken to see The Admirable Crichton by James Barrie—it was all of Peter Pan, Swiss Family Robinson and had all the charm of a well blown iridescent bubble. And then there were Walter Hampden and Fay Bainter.

Wrecked on the island for three years and the servant becomes the king, and the mistress becomes his charming servant and then his lover. And there on the island they are happy, until the call of a boat rescues them and shatters their class position and the romance.

And I wanted to be the king and I wanted you to be my slave (not really), my lover. "When I was a king in Babylon and you were my Christian slave" (in Jerusalem).

And we too shall be shipwrecked for a year or two or more—and we shall be carefree and gay and blow bubbles and live—just the two of us—until the ship (blast it) shall call us back to civilization. But we shall be full of the zest of living, free of the burden of civilization.

So I can almost jump upon the desk and sing,

> Tweedle de diddle deedee
> I am going out to sea
> To a very strange countree
> Where a princess waits for me
>
> We'll blow bubbles there all day
> Make dream worlds out of clay
> And sing and dance and play
> With backs to the world we'll say
>
> Tweedle de diddle dee dee
> At last we two are free
> Of the ties that bind, you see
> Tweedle de diddle de dee.

Here's a smile in the sun to a comerado—and I shall come before the green turns to grey—and then is when a comerado is needed—

My folks have moved to 1325 Lafayette Ave, Bronx, so write there.

Love,
Ellis

Ellis to Celia, March 22, 1931

Marca—

Tonight I miss you so and want you so—that Sept. seems years and years hence—despite the fact that the second moon shows a slender scimitar in the east.

I could come at once.

I will soon go to a lecture with a substitute, but it is so unsatisfying.

No longer "a substitute at a minute's notice" but "a substitute for a minute or so."

If I had money I would leave at once—

Goodnight dear comerado. I feel better for having talked to you.

Love

Ellis

Ellis to Celia, March 30, 1931

Lillian has come and I found in her the stardust that had gathered on her cloak from the companionship with my comerado. And as she spoke of you and the land, I scooped my hands full of the stardust that was on her and carried it away, knowing that my comerado had touched her with the vivacity and enthusiasm, with the sensitivity of a beautiful soul. And as I grasped her hand I thought of the hand of my comerado.

And I who talk so much, listened so well. But I was happy you hadn't come and I was sorry Lillian had come to Marks instead of Marks coming to Lillian—stardust can't live long in the cold city of New York. There is a smallness in the life of this city that will not nurture stardust.

It is so hard to wait and days drag intolerably. It is wise that I wait until September and add more to my meager store of gold.

I've heard of your new work, of your escapades and adventures and I am happy because of the exuberant ecstasy of my lovely Marca.

Lillian was happy and Marks was ecstatic at the return. But I fear the devastating effect of an ugly city.

Love has hit them deeply in the absence. Lillian arrived without the family's knowledge. And they spent the evening and night together at the

Hotel Piedmont on Piccadilly. Only I was let into the secret and Marks granted me an interview for two hours. This morning Lillian intended going home with a story of being detained at quarantine. How they have progressed—just disregard morals—and in N.Y.

And I feasted on pictures of you. Little you, big you, <u>fat</u> you (it was out of focus, Lillian explained, coming to your defense). And I wanted to go to you at once.

If I do not receive a better offer for camp—you will have me on your hands in June. I shall know more definitely next week. Perhaps we can find positions in Paris, Vienna, Italy or Istanbul, teaching English, selling books or anything.

Get moving Father Time—Marca waits for me.

Ellis

Ellis to Celia, April ___, 1931

This is the song of my coming to you—and the ringing of magical names in my ears—this is the call of a great desire of a rooted one for a comerado—This is the cry of dragging days and weeks that barely move.

Now if we had wealth—now if we had riches, I would strain and break the ties that bind and fly to the arms of my comerado.

All day I spent, reading and listening to the tales of Europe. I followed breathlessly the stories of adventures thru Europe—and I said to myself— if such was the glee and such was the charm of them, what will the charm be with my comerado.

Tell me comerado do days drag for you—are you too moulding dream hills that we can climb breathlessly?

'Tis strange about the pace of time.

It is strange how all my ambitions and aspirations have been drowned in the one big sea of my desire to go East and to you. To go without restrictions for as long as we want to. This time I shall be a

Prometheus Unbound—beware!

All this epistle has been written in moving subways on the way to three clubs on a very miserable rainy night.

Write me lots, dear, and tell me what to bring or send, where we will go, what I should wear, how shall I go, how much we will need, what you will do.

Write about our trip so that it will seem nearer.

But above all, write often.

My love to you

Chapter 18

Dearest far-away family
(Correspondence between Celia Antopolsky and her family,
April 4, 1931 to April 15, 1931)

Minna to Celia, April 4, 1931

Dearest Sister Celia,

First of all, I want to say that your letter, as letters go, was the most wonderful one that I have ever read. Secondly, the fact that it was written to me, and the revelation that I have a sister like you, makes me feel elated. All I can say is that your kid sister broke down and "bawled" like a two-year-old when she read it. And the necklace is one of the loveliest of any I've seen, and is the envy of all the girls. Everyone raves at how beautifully it is made and I'm delighted with it.

About my marriage—Mama and Papa have been simply marvelous about it. All is forgiven and they have grown to like Al very much. Papa gave us $200 toward our home, and as we had some too, we fixed up the nicest little 3 room apartment in a brand new house in the heart of Brownsville! What could be sweeter? (Incidentally I always hated Brownsville and vowed never to live there, but this place is ideal, since it is near both Mama's and Al's place of business). And Celia, we are very happy. Al is the most wonderful husband, and just because he happened to win a prize for interior decorating once, he can be seen walking around the house with a little can of colored enamel, painting little knobs and pipes and whatnot, breaking up what he calls "the monotony of one color."

ANDREA JACKSON

He certainly has added attraction to the place and he is always cleaning or polishing something. We have a darling home and I'm sure you'll love it.

Lillian looks beautiful. Such color! When she came, we almost went wild greeting her. Mama was a little sad because you didn't come with her. But they were crazy about the Haggadah [prayer book for Passover] and everything. Lillian hasn't her trunk and so they haven't seen the rest of the things you sent, but everyone was glad to <u>see</u> Lillian and <u>hear</u> about you.

Lillian came with her mother. [Minna means Lillian's stepmother.] She's a nice woman but she talks too much. She's been here to see Mama several times during the past winter. Poor Lillian will have to put up with a welcome home party and whatnot according to her mother. Lillian was silent but she saw sympathy in my face and we both understood. Mrs. Shapiro wanted Lillian to bring Marks to the Seder and all that. She said "Alright, you don't have to marry him, but bring him to the house. Celia was like that too, wasn't she, Mrs. Antopolsky? They're funny that way" and on and on until Lillian had to fairly pull her out of the house to go shopping for a Spring outfit. But all in all, we were glad to see Lillian, and the tales she told were all very interesting. You must be having a marvelous time and I'm glad.

And I'm glad I know you love me because I love you too, in fact behind all the battles we ever had I've always admired and loved you.

And now, won't you please write to us every now and then and if you will let me know when Ellis is sailing I can send you some dresses to come home in. I guess your supply of clothes has dwindled by now.

Al wants to write so I'll have to leave him some space. Au revoir,

Your loving sister,
Minnie

From Al:

Dear Celia:

I'm just a simple soul and have never been a wizard at expressing things but I do want to thank you for your beautiful letter and to tell you that I love Minnie with my whole heart and soul and will do anything within my power to make her happy. May peace and happiness be with you too—always.

Most sincerely,

Al

Letter dated April 10, 1931 from W. B. Robinson M.D., The Dr. Nathan Tucker Laboratory, Mt. Gilead, Ohio to Mrs. Sarah Antopolsky, Brooklyn, N.Y.)

Dear Madam:

We have your letter and are sending you by Ry. Ex. three ounces of Asthma Specific which are due on your original order. In future the medicine will be $1 per ounce.

Irving Antopolsky, Celia's brother, to Celia, April 11, 1931

Dear Sister Celia—

I ought to be shot, hung, or at least very severely reprimanded for my persistent neglect and continued failure to write letters, but the truth of the matter is, I've written at least fifty in my mind, merely to succumb to Old Man Procrastination.

To get down to business, I will relate, in my uninterested way, the happenings, events and occurrences concerning the Antopolsky family orchard, or I should say tree, some of which you may have heard of, but would bear repeating.

As far as health is concerned, everything is normal and satisfactory, and nothing for you to worry about. As to business and financial matters, same.

Now, you've heard about the marriage of our beloved sister, Minerva. Well, that episode has caused more anguish, comments, discussions and arguments, to say nothing of predictions, than anything else. You should have seen the drama enacted in our house, the day following Min's marriage, when the loving couple came in person to inform Mama and Papa, and also to take away Minna's personal belongings. No humor here, sister. Mama was in tears, Papa was cajoling Minna to stay home, and later storming about in his attempts to throw out the two of them; Betty, battling more because of some insult from Al, Min's husband, than for the lost cause; Joanie standing around, mute and rather frightened, Nat, full of sympathy, and myself feeling rotten, being angry with and sorry for Minna, at the same time. Minna, after many tears, left at last, and our home was actually in a state of mourning. Things have lightened, however, as you can't help but bow to the inevitable. I do want to say at this time, that there is nothing more cheering to Mama than one of your letters, which act as a tonic and actually make her feel good. You should write more often, although coming from me, the request is rather ironical.

Lily's arrival last week was a very pleasant surprise to us all. She came in looking fine, all loaded up with pictures and souvenirs, the latter, you may rest assured, being properly appreciated by family and myself. Kindly accept thanks, my thanks in advance, as I have not received my kimono yet, due to boat delay.

The Haggadah you sent Mom was very much fussed over at the first Seder (we had a real good one) and now occupies a place of honor with Mama's favorite chumish and machzer [Bible and holiday prayer book].

The rumor is that you intend to stay in Palestine until the end of August. Good luck to you if you do, as you're not missing very much in America.

I suppose you'd like to know whether you've received any mail or phone calls during your absence. Well, we did get quite a few calls from young men seeking your address, said requests all being duly complied with. A few letters have come from the Board of Education, one asking whether or not you wished to teach next fall and if so, what subjects.

I didn't answer that one. You might also be interested to know that there is a possibility of getting 75 to 100% of your money from the defunct Bank of U.S. Well, enough of this minor gossip and before closing, I request a personal letter addressed to your brother,

Irv

Celia to Antopolsky family, April 15, 1931, typed on office stationery

Dearest far-away family,

Here the heroine appears again, this time in a new light, as private secretary to the Lawrence T. Beck mentioned above. The scene is in the Old City of Jerusalem in the house of an aristocratic Arab family, which has temporarily evacuated in favour of the City Government. Sheikhs to the left of me, sheikhs to the right of me, blabbing in Arabic, onward they thunder—, learning a word or two, glad that I am a Jew, finally pulling through, onward I blunder—

But really, dear people, it is a fascinating job I have now, with an Arab boy to open the door for me, a wonderful cook to bring me tea, Turkish coffee, and delicious meals, a setting more romantic, much more, than a cheap novel, and me the only woman on the biggest engineering job in Jerusalem. One minute, I'm crouching on the floor helping my boss lay out a plan for the tunnel, the next I'm applying iodine to some poor workman's cut finger, the third minute I'm welcoming the Mayor of the city who has come down to see the Works, the fourth minute I'm entertaining the Department of Antiquities, the fifth minute I hear we have discovered a whole street from the time of King Herod, the sixth minute I'm dispatching a telegram to Egypt for more machinery, the seventh minute I'm telling an admirer on the 'phone that I can't see him tonight because I'm too busy, the eighth minute I'm interpreting between my boss and a German contractor, I using bad Yiddish for German, the ninth minute I'm taking down letters in shorthand as fast as possible, and the tenth minute, grand climax, I'm mending a rip in my boss's English tweed knickers. And that's only ten minutes out of a busy day, but, oh, how much I am learning that I could never learn in New York, and I shall be an expert secretary when I finish this job. Which is no small thing!

Lillian will tell you why it is that I can't leave now. I am living alone, in a charming room, with the family of a famous pianist in Jerusalem. I have many, many friends, and I am quite happy except now and then when I think of you all in New York and want to be back for a little while. I would love more than anything else to have a picture of you all. How does Mama look? Papa? And has Joanie grown much? Betty, please write. Irving, after all, I was your sister once. Why not let me know something of the new girl? As soon as I begin getting my salary and have bought some of the new clothes I need so badly, I shall be able to send home some of the lovely things there are in this wonderful old city. If it weren't for the difficulty of making money here, I would give anything to have our family come out to live in Palestine, but I am afraid to advise it under the present conditions. I am really very lucky to have a good job, as many are without employment. It is only now that I am appreciating all my experience in education and in meeting people. My job calls into play every latent ability of mine.

Dear people, I love you all and think of you many times in the day. Why, it will soon be almost a year that I have been away, but here with new experiences and places, the time seems to have flown. I want, more than anything else, a picture of mother and father.

Lovingly,
Celia

Work on the El Wad Sewer Project

Chapter 19

Smug complacency and stupid egotism

(Letters between Celia Antopolsky and Harry Neiman,
March 12, 1931 to June 1, 1931)

Celia to Harry, for hand delivery: given to Lillian on March 12, 1931,
as Lillian prepares to sail for America

Dear, dear Harry—

You must not wait too anxiously for me. I shall not be coming along until after the summer has passed. The fates and I have decreed it so, and there will be a long time for you to become famous and perhaps to marry.

You must pin no slightest hope to me. I am, after all, a will-o-the-wisp, never destined to stay long in any place, even a heart. I fly quickly always just managing to disentangle my feet that do get caught. The real "me" is never actually imprisoned. Let Lillian tell you more. Write to me, for I do like you. And oh good, good luck, Boy.

Forgive me!
Celia

Harry to Celia, April 3, 1931, stapled to letter above

Sevia Antopolska,

This prize piece of smug complacency and stupid egotism was delivered by Lillian to-day. Read it and be proud.

While, admittedly, I like Celia Antopolsky, the person, the friend, I do not like the conceited jackass with the perverted imagination that is the "artist" Sevia Antopolska (only <u>she</u> could have written such a letter) who steadily refuses to know, when she should know, quite finally and definitely (certainly we have been over the ground often enough) that I do not regard her as a sweetheart, and would not regard her as such were she entirely willing.

Under the circumstances, I think, wonderful, conceited, transient will-o-the-wisp with the good fortune to disentangle her feet from imaginary webs, this letter was misdirected. I have no doubt there are many proper recipients for it, and its like, somewhere else. That is why I ask you to take it back, and in return I will do as you say, "forgive you" although why you ask me to do so is just a little too subtle, even for me who know you so long.

I do not wish to hurt you, Celia, but please, do not let Sevia write such a letter again; if she must, let her pick on someone more deserving.

Best wishes,
Harry

Celia to Harry, May 3, 1931

Humbly, Harry; so humbly, that the pride and arrogance have gone out of me like frightened little children, I ask you to forgive me for that letter.

How can I tell you the circumstances in which I wrote it, the frenzied, hurried moment of Lillian's departure when I was torn between a wanting-to-go-with-her and the certainty of staying. What a funny, upset little note it is! As I read it again, in the warm bright sunlight here, I realize, as you say, that it was not meant for you at all but was merely a gesture of renunciation for all the dear things I have in America and the people I love there. But in it, haphazard and momentary as the message was, I have written my credo, though you have failed to recognize it, and this credo I send back to you as a memento of my brief, unimportant passage through your life. These are not words of bravado, dear Harry. They are the song the bird sings when morning breaks upon him, and his message in the evening when night wraps about his head.

"I am, after all, a will-o-the-wisp, never destined to stay long in any place, even a heart. I fly quickly, always just managing to disentangle my feet that do get caught. The real 'me' is never actually imprisoned."

And you, buried as you are in the tawdry conventionalisms of New York, for which I am sorry, choose to attribute to me the commonplace desire of the proverbial maid to taunt the proverbial man. Do you think for one moment that the thought of marriage or sweethearts or the other various items involved in St. Valentine's Day suggested itself to me?

Listen to me, Harry. My confidence was only in our friendship. I thought perhaps that you wanted me to come back as I have wanted you to come here. Had I looked forward to your coming, I should not have been ashamed of my eagerness, and had you failed me, I should have wanted a word of explanation.

I could love you for your hurt, angry, proud letter which is just about one hundred inches of Neiman chin going up, up. (Do you remember how you used to say, 'We'll go high someday'?) But it only makes me like you more. And if you don't answer my letter, I shall know that you saw a butterfly pass, and killed it to see what its wings were made of.

Celia

Harry to Celia, June 1, 1931 at the office 8 p.m.

Room 1705
291 Broadway
New York City, N.Y.
United States of America

Darling—

Your letter was timely, for ever since sending my letter I had forgotten yours, remembering only that I had written with intent to hurt you; that in doing so I had been nothing more than a little boy who, having sustained a supposed, perhaps imaginary, injury, had struck out blindly without caring who was hurt, nor how badly. Know this, dear, that I'd give a lot to erase, if that were possible, the moments, or hours, in which you may have been unhappy because of my letter!

Will you believe, sweet, that many times after it was written, and while I was hesitating for days before mailing, I did visualize and realize too, the circumstances and the reasons for the phraseology of your note, and that in the end, against my better judgment and common sense, I mailed it with misgivings? The small boy inside had taken advantage of a weak moment and won a victory. I move we forget it (the letter) and remember only the warm, joyous, happy times when we were grateful to the fates for knowing each other. I like to think there were such times and that they still are not of the past.

Of course, I was bitterly disappointed that you elected to stay in Palestine. It's hard not to be selfish about it, Celia, for we all, in one way and another, are benefited by your presence; but, forgive me if I sound stupid, just what is it that is keeping you there away from us—and me? I doubt whether you've ever been specific about it. I wonder, do you know yourself!

As for myself, there is so much and so little to write of. The most interesting is that I no longer spend sleepless, anxious nights just before a trial, but on the contrary, look forward with curiosity, without the taut, tense feeling which used to grip me, conjecturing upon the possible outcome: whether So and So will make a good witness, whether the story he will tell (most of the time it is only a story) will ring "true" to a jury composed, as they often are, of six or twelve, not so very clever, men. And some times I'm in doubt whether the former state of great excitement is not preferable to the blasé matter-of-fact attitude that is now mine.

Do not gather from this that I enjoy losing, far from it, but Celia, just between the two of us, when a client hires you in a vain attempt to relieve himself of a just obligation, you cannot, even if you are his lawyer, feel very deeply if he is unsuccessful. My sincere regret is that economics make it impossible for me to refuse to represent such a person in such a case. It is, without exception in my case, with a somewhat guilty feeling that I do take such work, promise to do my best and receive a few dollars as a fee, thus becoming an accessory, I think I may use that ugly word, to the client's dishonesty. Is there any wonder then, that the public generally have little respect for judges and almost none at all for lawyers?

If this picture is a gloomy one it is good to remember that sometimes, as last week, people come to you and say, "this is a very important matter to us. We want you to handle it, for we know that the first thing you think of is our interests and then of your fee while most lawyers reason the other way 'round." Celia, that _is_ a thrill. Almost as great as receiving a letter from Palestine. And also whenever, as at present, talk is rife of another investigation of the conduct of lawyers, it is good to sit back and calmly say, "Is that so, when do they start?" and not to feel a sudden pounding of the heart as needs must every filthy shyster of an ambulance-chasing lawyer in the city. And so, I'm glad not to feel like a mouse in constant fear of the cat. From this you must know, "I'm only a stranger here, Heaven is my home."

You know, from the new address, that I've moved. The change was a good one, I think, for now there is no rent, telephone, stenographer, clerk bugaboo hanging over me. Under this new arrangement I try a case or two each week for the lawyer with whom I'm associated and in return all my expenses are taken care of by him. It requires no more than 6 or 7 hours of my time each week and I save $80 or $85 a month; a saving that my family, unfortunately, have great need of, and the experience gained is always an asset.

I'm through talking shop.

This letter should have been written long ago, but I wanted to make it a long one and kept waiting for an appropriate time.

I haven't seen Lillian since meeting her shortly after her arrival months ago. I did promise to get in touch with her but do not know her address or 'phone number (there are so many Shapiro's in the 'phone book) and somehow, don't bother Harold for the information because after all, Lil and Marks must be quite busy with each other after the long separation, and I, well frankly, I'd never appreciate Marks's company if you were the one who'd come home and Lil remained away. Two's company and three's a crowd is hackneyed and prosaic, but you can't beat it for hard, common sense and diagnosis of the state of mind of people suffering as I think they are.

Some time ago you asked me to send you another picture. I'll take one one of these days and mail it to you. I can't afford to have you forget what I look like; not if you stay amongst so many, I understand, handsome, idealistic, intellectual, fortune hunting, adventure seeking (what-have-you) Lochinvars, in a land where one doesn't need much money, where the "nights are full of romance" (quotations yours).

You warned me that my not answering your letter would mean so very serious a thing. My crime, dear, would be a great one, for I would be turning from the only friendship that I've had with a girl which was genuinely spontaneous and free, joyously and openly unreserved and real. I intend to hold it tightly, very closely, very long. Write to me soon.

Harry

Chapter 20

Please, Celia—destroy this letter

(Correspondence between Lillian Shapiro and Celia Antopolsky,
March 20, 1931 to April 27, 1931)

Lillian to Celia, March 20, 1931, mailed from Cherbourg, France

Dear Celia, who remains in the land of blue skies,

Once having been in Palestine, I am continually conscious of the lack of Palestinian qualities in atmosphere. Not one day since I left the Mediterranean has been blessed with the sun from morning through to evening; and although I came into Paris with the sun rise, it is drizzling now.

First, thank you so much for your birthday greetings. They meant a welcome to me on entering Paris.

I have a queer feeling on this whole trip that my experiences are not new; each place is so well known to me through so many connections that it seems like an old friend seen in a new light.

My impression of Italy is that of an intimate country. Even its language is soft sounding and has many diminutives for each word. In the south, the olive, peach, and almond trees were in full bloom. Oxen pulled the two wheeled carts—the oxen are all white. The south of Italy is a warm green, but as we zigzagged across the country northward, the weather was colder, the trees bare, and acres on acres of tall grape trees were evidence of Italy's wine supply.

Mussolini has his country organized in a military (psychological) state of mind. First, the police (the Fascisti) secure complete allegiance to Il Duce. They are attractively dressed in Lincoln green knickers, black shirts, purple and gold ties, green jackets, Peter Pan hats including the feather, and a revolver very much in evidence. They are everywhere. Then there are the soldiers and cadets (a stupid lot who are certain that they are the "olive oil" of Italy but who know as little as a N.Y. policeman). They are however given a severe course of "military" training. They, too, are attractively dressed in blue suits, brass buttons, long blue capes lined with red, swords, three cornered hats or perhaps a plumed affair (depending on the rank). It is true that Italy is much cleaner than I expected.

Rome is made up of various squares ("piazzas") where Rome's heroes have a chance to be immortalized, but after I went through the Vatican museums, miles in length, I was convinced that entirely too many Romans had the Palestinian urge for reproduction of their physiognomies.

(Continued March 24, 1931)

Florence is a lovely place, with very much of the Renaissance life in evidence, because of the churches (you remember the famous doors of the Baptistry—they are beautiful), the palaces and their secret entrances and rooms for alchemists which are decorated by Leonardo, Donatello, Botticelli, etc., etc.

At night, on the street bordering the Po River, a young man serenaded with a guitar to a shuttered window above. He wore an opera cloak and really had a good voice.

Until Venice, the Polish girl accompanied me. I was happy when she left. She was a "nouveau riche,"—her grandfather in Palestine left her money. She criticized Palestine for its lack of culture, admired a dress with the same enthusiasm as the Medici tomb, ate macaroni and soup with awful table manners, and had two white-gold teeth. 's enuf, n'est-ce pas? I am afraid that we are both spoiled for other people—to live with, I mean. As a matter of fact, I don't believe I could live with another girl now.

In Paris, I wandered around town by myself first, to get the lay of the land, and then with Riva's neighbor, Miriam Frankel, who was on the boat with me. With her and her friends, I saw a good deal of Paris. They live in the Latin Quarter. First, we went riding at night, in a taxi, along the beautiful boulevards, attractively lit up. The sky of Paris is red at night, and the architecture, being Baroque, makes the city look like a city of windows and lights.

The cafes in Montparnasse have some good music. With a Roumanian, I heard an excellent Balalaika orchestra. The traditional thing I did was to go to the very top of the Eiffel Tower, from where Paris looks like Lilliput, with a toy river, toy bridges, and puppets for people. I did not, however, go into the Louvre. I had sufficient of museums for the present. I did see, instead, the old Montmartre, some old cafes where entertainment is provided to the French in the same manner as at the time of the French Revolution, the revue that features Josephine Baker, the coloured actress who took Paris by storm a year or two ago (the Follies Bergere was closed so I saw it not), and wandered about on both sides of the river, in artists' quarters and out.

I must go for the baggage now. Write.

Love,
Lillian

Lillian to Celia, April 1, 1931, New York

Dear Celia,

A joyous Pesach [Passover] to you tonight, and much happiness for many, many years.

I, myself, am very happy, really so! These two days I am here have been so full that I am still walking on air.

No one knew I was coming, except Joey, and even he was not certain —letters are still coming in which I wrote to my family in Europe. Therefore, my arrival was quite a surprise which resulted in an enthusiastic reception. The boat was delayed about 10 hours because of a heavy fog— but I saw Ellis about two hours after I arrived.

All of his energy and plans are focused on seeing you. From my description of Palestine, he is undecided as to whether he should leave before or after camp. His waiting until September would give him the advantage of building up his health, physically, and of an additional few hundred in cash, which is essential, you know. He wants to write to Berkson again about a job in Palestine (if he only knew Hebrew, he might possibly get Grossman's job).

Ellis says that when he leaves the country, it will be with no time limit for returning—perhaps not at all. If I were you, I would write him, spurring him on to complete his thesis, and telling him how much a degree means in Palestine. His plans are so much taken up with the future that he is apt to neglect the present.

I saw your family. Your mother and father are, of course, very much disappointed at your not coming back for Passover. I cheered them up considerably by my stories of you, your job, and Palestine. They were thrilled with the gifts and letters, especially Minna, who wept at reading your note to her. She was home, in your house, learning cooking. She has her own home which she has furnished, and she tells me she is happy for the first time in years.

Do write to them, Celia, and often. They had not received a letter from you in three weeks. Your mother saves all the pressed flowers you send her; and send her some recent pictures.

She has had a hard winter—been ill, and she is pale and weak. You don't know what a difference a letter from you makes. (They were afraid you were ill).

Irving looks well; he is successful in his studies this year, and is quite a well-dressed young man. He has a good deal of poise.

I have not yet seen or done any of the 101 things I must do within the next week or two.

As far as work is concerned, jobs are extremely scarce. I shall make a few dollars immediately after Easter by substituting, and meanwhile look about for an interesting position, if any are available.

Write me the truth about how you feel about staying on. If you intend staying away another year, I think you ought to get a visit in to your mother somehow. It would replenish her store of strength.

I hardly need mention the fact that Ellis sends his love. (Many times he sought out Joey to talk of you). Best regards to you from your family, Joey, my brother, etc., and from me to Jerusalemites.

Shalom,

Lillian

Celia to Lillian, April 9, 1931, typed on stationery from the City Engineer's Department, Municipality of Jerusalem; Tel. No. Jerusalem 681; Construction Manager, El Wad Sewer Reconstruction, Lawrence T. Beck A.M.I.C.E.

Our Reference No. Chaverah b'Yerushalaim [girlfriend in Jerusalem]

Dearest Lillinka,

I have so much to say to you that I really don't dare begin, and it was with that procrastinating thought in mind, that I have not yet written to you at length. But I do begin, firmly, decisively, as becomes one who lives altogether alone (? judging from the number of my visitors) and is the very private secretary of the above-mentioned Construction Manager.

Last night, I danced at the student's dance, Palace Hotel, until 3 A.M. All our friends and many others were there, and I, in my delicate green chiffon dress which you have seen too often (alas!), said green dress having had its tan collar removed leaving it sleeveless and the bosom embellished with soft pink blossoms, created the usual furore. I am becoming so popular that I count as precious the few minutes I have alone. Turning on the light in my room is the signal for people to come visiting and they do come, at all hours, so that I am as usual on the verge of a few heart affairs. The most interesting at the moment is a fine young fellow, <u>tall</u>, really handsome, and with all the glamour of having been through pogroms, the Russian Revolution, and a few other catastrophes. To add to that, he has just returned from the desert where he has been studying Bedouin folk lore about which he is about to publish a book. Moreover, he has fallen for the undersigned with a well-known thump, and he speaks and understands English, and he knows books, and life looms interestingly once more. Mayor and Asch are still somewhere in the offing; Reis, Zuker, and Grossman still frequent Patt's and the Vienna; the weather is altogether delightful; and many people ask for news of you.

This morning, as I was strolling to work, a little girl ran after me with a pathetic query, "Why Miss Shapiro not come?" What could I do but stifle a little heartache and answer, "Miss Shapiro b'America."

Write to me, dear child. Tell me if you are happy as I want you to be. Do be good and let me know the exact status of my family. And I depend on you to send me a pretty white sport dress, a long frock I might wear in the evening, my evening dress and velvet jacket, some silk stockings, a few Woolworth accessories, and <u>news</u>! Go to see Pater, will you? [publisher of "The Poet and the Critic"]. A check from him would help a lot. I haven't had a moment to do Mr. Beck's private work, but my salary here has been raised to LP12 [12 Palestinian pounds] and everyone is generally pleased with my efficiency. There!

My great love to <u>you</u>, Joey Marks, Ellis, of course my family and yours.
—Yours, Celia

Lillian to Celia, April 9–6, 1931

> April 9, 1931
> In the park behind the 42nd Street library—the grass is sprouting green and the benches are completely covered by their spring occupants

Dear Celia,

It is a week since I have written, during which I am picking up threads, both old and new. New York, itself, has improved its skyline considerably. The Empire State building is an imposing structure because of its simplicity. The economic situation is bad—everywhere there are bankruptcies and dismissal of employees, but somehow, the New York girl manages to be well-dressed, prices are reduced considerably, and the feeling is that "the worm must turn."

Within the last two days, your family and Ellis called to discover if I had news from you—I had not, and no-one has received word for three weeks.

I suppose you have heard of the shock your family had. Your uncle, Kale's husband, died suddenly, immediately after a Pesach dinner. Betty felt badly about it because she felt that Kale and Bach Yussel were two of the few people in your family who had been happy together. I have not seen your mother since so I do not know how it affected her.

Ellis' call was with more cheerful news. He expects to leave definitely about June 15th, and go to the Zionist Congress first. He is spending his time between steamship offices and reading books on "How to Go to Europe for Next to Nothing."

I saw Reici's friend, Rose Landis. I shall lunch with her tomorrow and see the head of her organization where she thinks there may be a vacancy in social work.

Next day

I did lunch with Rose. She is quite a fine girl. She is head of the department of Home Economics of the United Jewish Aid Society in Brooklyn where, Miss Antopolsky, I begin work on Monday.

Financially, the position is not very lucrative <u>now</u>, because I enter as a <u>trainee</u> for three months during which I take courses at the New School for Social Work and learn the practical procedure of Family Case Work. The head of the organization was so keen on getting me in that he offered me $100 a month for the period of training, more than any one else was ever given by the organization. Family Case Work is necessary as a basis for all Social Service work and I feel I shall get a good deal of satisfaction out of it.

I went to see Harry Neiman. (Next time you write to him, spell his name correctly, whichever way is the correct one). You were entirely mistaken about his attitude toward you, and your note hurt him considerably, since you implied that he is waiting for you, whereas he feels that there is no basis for your assumption. We had had a very pleasant conversation in which he told me of his work and I told him of Palestine. When he opened your note, he expected a cheerful, light note, humorous perhaps. I myself had quite forgotten the contents. He was completely astonished by the tone and implication. He was in the process of moving (to 291 Broadway) and was quite confident in himself. He does not deny that he has missed you, but he does not think that either of you would be happy married to one another. I spent ½ hour explaining the circumstances under which you wrote the note, your psychology as you finished your letters home etc. He prefers not to have the matter mentioned again. Write him a cheerful, light letter.

I have been tracing Pater around town. He has moved, and has no regular office. He receives mail in Rm. 610, 7 E 42nd Street, where there is no information regarding any other address. All that is known of him is that he calls once a day for his mail. Joey left his business card asking to be called by telephone at his office—no response. There has been no further issue of the magazine, according to anyone's knowledge. The chap must be quite "broke."

The trunk arrived. I brought the stuff you sent to your house. Your mother is "antzict" [thrilled] with the shawl; Betty is thoroughly convinced that you are her dear sister, from the gifts to Joanie and herself. Your mother looked and felt very much better, and did not speak of your returning so soon. She would not be displeased if you married in Palestine and she were to come out there.

Good luck and write your plans!

Regards to Emma, and the Patt's Eating Circle.

Lillian to Celia, April 27, 1931 (arrived Jerusalem postmark May 12)

Dearest Celia,

Your letter gave me a twinge of homesickness for my chaverah b'Yerushaliam. Oh for a magic carpet or an Aladdin's lamp with a round trip wish for either of us.

Your new conquest sounds attractive. Have you fallen for him too or are you going to add another catastrophe to his list?

I was to see your mother today, and I read her that part which suggested you were not entirely alone. It pleased her, but your father wanted to know why he received no letters. Your mother's health is fluctuating—write to her often. (This is part of my social service work). It is amusing to see me sitting in Brownsville houses, listening to old and young women's tales of woe. They generally bless me, my friends, and my family—so that you, too, are included from hence until "Meshiach" [until the Messiah comes].

I have spent beautiful, perfect days with Joey. All his charm is here, with an additional depth and self-confidence—and you know how charming he can be.

Next evening, in the 42nd
street library

Dearest Girl,

I have been thinking things over, and decided that in order to be fair to you, I must present a full picture, and not part of it, as I have done re: Ellis. Always, the trouble with your relationship was that you had only one side of the picture, and I hate so much to have you disappointed later or made the least bit unhappy when it might really matter, that I shall tell you the situation as I know it—because if I don't, who will? It may make no difference to you to know the whole picture, but whether it does or not, I can risk the feeling that it is a breach of etiquette on my part to Ellis.

What I wrote you about Ellis's enthusiasm is true. At the same time, since Ellis's Buffalo trip with Lee, they have been sharing an apartment in Brooklyn Heights, a charming place. It may be for convenience, of course. I suspect that Lee foots the bills, while Ellis is saving his money. However, in order to make it right before the world, the rumour was spread (by Moe, I believe) that Ellis and Lee were married in Buffalo. Personally, I don't believe they are. Joey and I were up there twice. The first time Moe, Lolly, Lee's brother, sister-in-law, etc. were there. Lee was very hospitable to me, and asked about Palestine. She invited us, again, one night for dinner, when Tyl, her husband, Ellis, Joey, and myself were there. Lee had cooked a rather good meal. (You see, I am trying to be objective). She is a good sport; you know that.

But why the devil couldn't Ellis write you this instead of my having to write it!

Then—Ellis's accomplishments for the year are his decision to go to Palestine and saving money for it. He did not write his thesis and he did not study Hebrew.

I am not attempting to decide what Lee's attitude toward Ellis's Palestinian trip is. You know that Ellis bought a round trip ticket—good for two years. And I am not attempting to say what Ellis really thinks of it. I don't know.

Believe me Celia, I want you to be happy above all else, but you must be fully conscious of things before you make your decisions. If you can be happier with any of our Palestinian "conquests" don't give it up. Do think of yourself! Because I believe that Ellis thinks of himself.

Perhaps I am wrong in writing all this to you. But unfortunately I am not a lover of subterfuge.

When I first heard Ellis was going, I was glad. Now, I am not so sure I am, because it means further complications for you.

Please don't interpret this in the sense of any antagonism to Ellis; I feel none except as concerns you. His sins against friendship are not commission, but omission.

And please, Celia—destroy this letter. You must understand that I don't wish this information mentioned to Ellis or anyone. Let him tell it of his own accord, if he so wishes.

Do write to me often!

Be joyous with the land—Shalom v'brucha [peace and blessings]

Lillian

Chapter 21

I am sincere in my emotions
(Letters from Ellis Polonsky to Celia Antopolsky,
April 6, 1931 to July 1931)

Ellis to Celia, April 6, 1931

Marca—

I am sorely troubled—more than three weeks have passed and there
has been no word from you, outside of a note delivered by Lillian. Twenty-
five days and no word from a comerado is ominous.

You are well tho, aren't you Marca? It is forgetfulness, business or even
disinterest, but nothing more serious. Your silence has thrown a muffler
over the enthusiasm that should be unbridled.

And today came to us meager reports of two men and a woman slain
in the Emek [this incident is mentioned in Chapter 7] and I am troubled.
What has silenced the song of my comerado to me? And here, I want to
rejoice and tell you lovely things, but my hand is hesitant to express my
heart when my comerado remains silent.

If you have lost interest in your comerado—read no further—If you
have forgotten him—read no further. If you are longing for him, ill or
troubled—read on—

Marca, I am coming in less than two months—coming to you—if
you'll have me. I knew that camp would be long and unbearable and I am
missing my comerado—I have turned my back to the money they offer
and turned my face to my comerado—if my comerado will have it.

I shall come with little money but great enthusiasm. Nine weeks from now—less than seven from the time you read this.

I am going to the Zionist Congress in Basle—June 29—can you come too? Then to Palestine.

How I want to be free, happy and unrestrained in this adventure and trip—but I find even now in writing is the miserable gap of a yawning hole of doubt of more than thee weeks' silence.

I am uneasy for word of my comerado. Perhaps one or two letters have been lost in transit. Are you writing to 1325 Lafayette Ave., Bronx?

Lillian is fast adjusting to the rigorous life of this ugly city.

I am coming soon—so soon Marca—and I am saving things to tell you and we shall walk arm and arm through the world. Do you hear me Marca—next moon is the fourth moon of our longing—

Love,
Ellis

Ellis to Celia, April 14, 1931

Marca—my own comerado—

When we had given up hopes of you and your friends and family had mourned you—and I in desperation had inquired about cable rates and had worded the cable, deciding I would give you another day—word came from you after the lapse of a month—and I wondered how a comerado—even such a businesslike and efficient one could be silent in the face of the longing of another comerado for so long. But I must forgive you.

I am not impressed—Not even six foot, silent slaves can elevate a secretary of sewers. It is a lowly and underworld profession and it just flows with filth—oh well.

But I for my part, comerado, I God's real assistant, have uttered magic words and lo, months have passed. Only yesterday I purchased my tickets and the date of sailing is June 20 and the boat is the Europa. Cherbourg and Paree—25th. Basle for the Congress—29. And a ticket to Trieste.

Today I plan to go to the doctor for an examination, overhauling and injections. Tomorrow I expect to get my passport—so all these things help time move a bit faster and June 20 a bit nearer. And my comerado a bit closer.

Listen, Marca, you can't work forever. Meet me at the station in Paris on the 25th of June. The station where trains from Cherbourg come. There should be special excursion fares to Paree because of some Colonial Exhibition they are planning. [Paris Colonial Exposition, 1931].

We can spend three days in Paree—then on to Basle for the historic [Zionist] Congress and then if money permits, trips through Italy, maybe the Black Forest of Germany or East to Constantinople, or who knows where.

Think of it, Marca—July and August have been added to our vacation— even if our budget is diminished considerably. Marca, I could roam through the strangest lands with you—

Oh how good it is. With years ahead and a sturdy comerado at my side, there is a world to see and a life to live.

It was true what I said, Lillian has lost the stardust of her adventure, the city has shaken it from her and she looks and acts less exuberant and exuberantly than she did when first she came.

She found a position in social work.

Do you believe me now, Marca, I have my ticket. Deck C—883—Europa.

Write and write in details.

Love,

Ellis

Ellis to Celia, April 16, 1931

Marca—

Why do you write so infrequently? Are you so absorbed by sewers?

Days are spinning madly for me. I am a real traveler. I have seen my dentist and he said the teeth are ready for the trip—I have seen my doctor and he said the body is ready—and God knows the soul is.

Yesterday I crashed thru crowds to see my bunk in the Europa, so that when I get there on June 20 I shall feel at home.

Now for my passport and visa—visas are more difficult to get—thanks to Simpson.

Together, France, Italy, Switzerland and Palestine—O—Marca—I cannot wait the meager moon or two.

Goodnight my comerado—write—
Love
Ellis

When shall I meet you?

Ellis to Celia, April 27, 1931 (arrived Jerusalem postmark May 26, 1931)

Marca Mia—

Your typewritten missive has finally come to me after a lapse. I guess I must be resigned to one letter in two weeks. But it is so good to hear from you, you who I shall be seeing before the third moon comes round.

This is the second time in as many letters that you insist on impressing me with the fact that I must not take anything for granted in so far as our relationship goes, when I come to you. Marca, my dear one, please do not fear, I shall expect no affection from you more than you shall have for me. "Things and people have come between us" you say. Of course my comerado and I should not have wanted to prevent that.

Remember, my dear girl—even if my letters do sound or promise a certain degree of dependence, I shall come expecting nothing or demanding nothing. You shall remain free of any entangling alliances, as far as I am concerned. So please my good companion, do not be troubled over my coming. You know that I understand and I too am a trifle sensitive—and I shall know if you want me near or far. And even in little Jerusalem we can be miles apart.

I swear to you, dear, dear girl that I am neither angry, nor hurt and I know that comerado and comerado shall go happily hand in hand in search of the sun. I bring you no chains but a smile in the sun, a light heart and a yearning comerado. It will be enough if I can hold your hand and whisper in your ear "Marca Mia" and then go.

All America comes to Basle and Palestine, two <u>Young Judaeans</u> are coming in the same boat—besides a Miss Chervish of National Fund.

I am so impatient to know whether you are to come to the continent, if so where and when? Your last letter does not indicate any knowledge of my latest intentions.

By the time you read this I shall be a mere four weeks from Europe— Do write—love if you'll have it.

Ellis

Ellis to Celia, May 5, 1931, Jerusalem postmark May 21

Listen!

A gray shadow casts itself before the sunshine of my hopes—a threatening spot looms in the horizon of my dreams—and she that was my comerado has called me "weakling."

Let the sunshine of my hopes assure her, let the horizon of my dreams make clear to her—that I need no prop of support, that unaided I can still climb hills—unsupported I can wander in search of a sunset.

Listen Celia, that was Marca, again your letter bears the tale of a fear that I shall not find you loving me; a warning that trees may shrivel in a year's space. And it comes to me the thought that trees may shrivel more from worry than from loneliness.

Please be at ease—I am not coming to the Land to pluck you from the soil or form the life about you—I am not coming to rest leisurely under the shade of your profuse foliage. I am coming home, dear girl.

I am coming to a land I love, I am coming to the fulfillment of a dream, a dream of a decade and a hope of a lifetime.

Go on with your pastimes and your comrades, fear me not as an intruder.

You that were my comerado and knew me well—what has happened to you? Have I ever stood between you and others, have I ever cried for you to turn your face to me <u>alone</u>? Do I that was your comerado appear to you as one that cringes and cries for support?

O Marca, for you are Marca, I am sorry for all this. Let us sit down and talk things out as we used to do. It was hard to read three letters, one after the other, tempered with the persistent fear that I might claim too much of you.

Months previously you wrote affectionately of a dream of doing the things you do together. Your hopes, your wishes but doubted that I would come to the Land. I caught the spark of your letters, I fanned the flame higher—I saw the way and I followed it. I was coming.

With a suddenness your desire to stay forever changed to a desire to stay for Passover—but you would wait through the hot summer for your comerado for a period that seemed years long.

The waiting seemed long for me too, a Zionist Congress sharpened the edge of my desire and I flung better judgment to the wind in the desire to see my land and my comerado.

Then came letters that portrayed the conflict of your emotions. You told me once that I must not be certain of your affection for me, you told me twice that one's feeling may change, you told me thrice that you could promise me nothing in respect to affection.

Has your comerado made claims upon you? Has he asked for affection? Has he been a jealous companion?

I want beauty, I want a cause, I want a hill, I want a cleansing sun, a free heart, a dream to dream and a comerado.

Forgive me if my earlier letters have climbed hills with you—if they have found bivouacs for us, if they have taken you thru strange streets and cities. Forgive me if the letters have boyishly dreamed weird fantastic scenes. They were no threats, they are not pledges, they are just unreal, whimsy dream stuff.

Understand Marca, I am not angry, I merely regret that I have troubled you so, that you need reiterate a fear that had no basis in fact.

There will come beautiful days and there will be mountains and hills to climb—and I shall turn to you and say

"I shan't be gone long

You come too"

And if Marca says "yes" we shall sing in the face of the sun and go but if Marca says "no," I shall grasp my knapsack and be off—and I shall understand and be neither hurt nor alone—for there is a road and the sun and beauty at the top.

I do understand that all of your fears have arisen because of the greater fear that you may cause me disappointment and suffering. You are a dear girl for it and I love you (if I may). But yours is a sturdy comerado and he is an understanding one.

It is beautiful spring in America and I leave in six weeks from Friday. I am glad we talked so long, now we can feel better.

"Shall we climb that hill?"

Your comerado
Ellis

Ellis to Celia, June 3, 1931

Marca—

The "Europe" leaves for its last voyage before it comes back for me— and I—I am all in readiness for the trip—passport, enthusiasm and the meager bank account.

Where to stay? What to see? How to go! have made waiting bearable. Inoculations and vaccinations have made waiting painful. I shall be the best inoculated man in the East.

As the day approaches, the party of tourists increases, and that is not my fault—I've done all I could to discourage travelling companions, but they insist on coming along.

The Congress program has just been published and sessions continue until July 10th, which means that sessions being interesting, I shall probably catch the boat the next Wednesday at Trieste and I'll be set—face Eastward for home.

I have had no word from you for weeks and I assume you are having a thrilling time and that you are so absorbed in living that you have no time for writing.

I am taking the privilege of sending some bulky things for me in care of you. I'm certain you will have no difficulty explaining the arrival of men's furnishings—tell them, "It's just a friend."

When I get to Palestine I should like to make the rounds "on foot" if possible to see the country and them what lives in it. It would be nice if you could and wanted to, come along.

So the revised schedule reads

> June 20—12.01 a.m. leave New York
> June 25—Cherbourg
> June 26, 27, 28, 29—Paris
> June 30 to July 10—Basle
> July 11 to 15 Somewhere in Italy
> July 15—Trieste
> July 20—Palestine—Jaffa
> (Schedule subject to change without notice)

Young Judaea here begins to bubble a bit with receptions for department members—and I just rarin' to go.

So, if God is willing, and the bank doesn't fail—I'll be "en voyage" by the time you read this.

I shall keep you posted when I can.

Until we meet again
Ellis
I'm coming

Ellis to Celia, June 11, 1931

Marca—Marquita –

Come Marca, you do know what a comerado means, don't you? and you have no faith or fear in the rabid rumors you hear because you know, my perplexed Marca, that soon you shall know from my own lips all that you wish.

You do know, my little girl, that despite all else I am sincere in my emotions, and I, this moment am so impatient to be near you, hold you so securely that you could feel secure, tell you things that you would be more certain of your emotions and mine.

Yes, I will tell you that my impatience and sudden decision to come to Palestine was because I missed you so. My coming to Palestine was assured fifteen years ago when I as a child felt the pang of homelessness, but my coming today instead of tomorrow was because you were there. Marca, if I want you and I leave all else to come to you, what else matters (if you want me to come?). If I leave all ties with no promise of return and I turn towards you, what else matters?

They have whispered before and you suffered; you dried your eyes and were ashamed. Now when they whisper, be at ease, know that I say it, "I am coming to you." My action belies their whispering. Come my little Marca, do smile again. I do want you happy, more than I want you—and I want you—if you want me to.

Make no complexities in your emotions, make no conflicts in your desires—do simply what you will and do not anticipate or search the past. There is beauty and joy in simple emotions.

But come give me your hand—I need no past Madison Colony [the Apartment], I need not haunt my two best friends in the trails of dead leaves. There are green leaves in the future and a blazing sun—a hill to climb, a comerado at one's side, a book—and Whitman is more Whitman with us than with any others. This only if you will.

But if you do not will it, <u>We can be friends</u>.

Somehow that sentence sounds worse than "We can be enemies." But we can be friends, I suppose, and I can have come for the country alone—and we shall go our way with a kindly nod, and a fleeting, musing thought—"of ashes that once were singing gold." And you, undisturbed, will live your social life, cheerfully and forgetting, save for a glimpse of me, a momentary pang—they soon, too, shall be less frequent—and time and circumstance will engulf the camaraderie—all this if you will <u>not</u>—

Do say that you <u>will</u>—you can say it to me c/o Zionist Congress, Muster-messe, Basle, Switzerland—you can say it to me at the Port of Jaffa, you can say it to me at Damascus Gate, you can whisper it to me on the Wall—

Your Land, my Marca—whether you will—or whether you will not. With you lies the future. (How dramatic!)

Now, while you read, I am in Paris (God willing)—Tuesday I shall be in Basle—Soon, O Lord soon, in Jerusalem. Marca—Marquita—you will be glad to see me—won't you—

Say that you <u>will</u>
Ellis

Ellis to Celia, June 25, 1931

Marca,

You are so near to me this moment—Whitman, Millay, Frost have called you back to me.

Marca Mia, (be that for a moment) I have just read your poems to a charming and appreciative travelling companion, Miss Levin of Cleveland, whom I discovered to be on board ship. She has written some very acceptable stories and is a really sensitive soul. I like her because she reminds me of you.

I read her poems of yours from The Poet and Critic and as I read them I came so close to you. When I finished we were both silent and she said to me "You love her, don't you?"

And I spent the day in Poetry and I went down the "Open Road" with you and Walt.

I cannot write Marca, I must whisper all that I want to say to you. Come give me your hand, I want to hold and be so near to you.

I am coming Marca, on the wings of longing. Cherbourg tomorrow, Paris, Basle, Trieste—Jerusalem. Will you open the gates for me.

I love my comerado
Ellis

Ellis to Celia, from Paris, June 29, 1931

Marca—

I have spent long and happy days in Paris. Versailles was made for kings but even a plebian like I am can be enraptured with it. And the Louvre, comerado—how you would have enjoyed the wealth of its treasures. How we would have searched breathlessly for the Mona Lisa, the soft, fine Mona Lisa hand in hand as we went on one occasion. It was dazzling, bewildering, almost impossible to digest the art in so short a time. One should spend a year in the Louvre and twenty in Paris.

I have so much to tell you, Marca, if you wish to hear. I had hoped you would have written to Paris telling me "you will." No word has come—and the American Express rarely loses mail.

So—I shall come soon, Marca—and you need not be troubled by me. I shall walk among you if not with you. I shall whisper if not to you. I shall be the ashes that once were singing gold.

So be at ease, I have read your eloquent message in the silence of four weeks. I come to stake no claims or reclaim no losses.

But Marca above all be honest with me and I shall be a great friend of yours. I am sure it can be so—I am sure, if you wish, I can walk beside you if not with you.

I have lived delightful years this week—I have opened new vistas that lead God knows where. I have read poetry—and found it living—

Marca—I tell you beauty has come back to me with the speed and certainty of eagle wings. Oh I can soar Marca—I can soar—my back is to the past—my face to the future—will you come too—

Ellis

Ellis to Celia, July 10, 1931, from Milan

Marca—

I have looked up to the mountains of Switzerland—I have looked down upon the cities of Switzerland—and I have found it good.

Time and again I have turned towards the East and primed myself for a call—the silence has stricken me mute.

I am leaving from Trieste definitely next Wed. and I will arrive in Jaffa on the 20th on S. S. Canora.

Are there hills in Palestine, comerado?

Ellis

Postcard from Ellis to Celia from Lucerne, picture of Swiss mountains. Date obscured: July __, 1931.

Marca—

There is a majesty in hills that makes one walk straight.
Am leaving for Palestine on 15th. Will arrive Jaffa 20th.
Shall I see you?

Ellis

Chapter 22

You see, we really want you to come home
(Correspondence between Celia Antopolsky and her family,
April 17, 1931 to September 24, 1931)

Mama Antopolsky to Celia, April 17, 1931 (in Irving's hand)

Dearest daughter Celia:

We were glad to see Lillian but we were grieved that you didn't come.

We were all delighted with your presents. The shawl is beautiful and we had a lot of fun trying everything on. Papa put on the robe and tied a towel around his head for a turban and walked around as an Arab. We almost died laughing. We thank you very much dear daughter, for the beautiful presents you sent us.

After Lillian told us how wonderful it is in Palestine, Papa and I were wishing that we could take a trip there. We want to know if you intend to come home or if you are going to stay there indefinitely. We are getting lonesome for you. Your friend Harry Neiman calls us quite often to inquire after you and also about my health. He seems very nice.

Please don't feel bad because I don't write to you so often. You know that if I could write I would write 3 or 4 letters a week, but as it is I have to coax one or the other of the children to write for me. But I want you to know that I am dictating every word of this letter myself.

Joanie is very sweet and is very intelligent. She has a wonderful imagination and is wise beyond her years. She was delighted with the little dress. Betty won't let her play with the doll. She uses the doll for an ornament.

Please write us more often and tell me about yourself.

Your loving
Mother

Celia to Mama and Papa, April 24, 1931

My beloved Mother and Father,

How I wish I could see you now! I should like to make a flying trip to America and then come back <u>quick</u> to Palestine, bringing you all with me. There is a peace here, in the quiet hills, in the old, old stones, that can be found nowhere in America. Sometimes I stop and listen for the noise of a city but there is no such noise. I hear perhaps, the music of birds, the braying of a donkey, or a rooster crowing. Our Jaffa Road is a real main street, and there are no numbers on any of the houses here. What, you want Ussishkin's house? Follow that narrow winding path all the way around until you come to an open field, cross it to the wide road leading to Rehavia Quarter, follow that etc., etc., and then ask for Ussishkin's house. Anyone knows it. And that's an address.

Do you remember I told you about a poem I translated on board ship? Well, Ussishkin, on his way back from America, saw Schneur the poet, in Paris, and Schneur, who was very much pleased with the poem, has sent me a letter. Interesting, isn't it?

Meanwhile, I still mingle in Jerusalem politics. It is amusing to think that an increase in my salary is being held up because the Mayor has not yet approved it. This morning Keith-Roach, the governor of Jerusalem, is coming to visit our Works and on Tuesday, the High Commissioner. With something new happening each day, I find it hard to be bored.

I wish Betty or Minna or Irving would write. I am hungry for news of home. The first word I have received in months is from Lillian.

Be well and happy, all of you. Betty, send some snapshots of Joanie, Mother and the others. Joanie must be lovely by now. Did the dress fit her?

I'll write again soon.

Love and regards,
Celia

Mama to Celia "dictated word for word by Mama," May 1, 1931

Dear Daughter:

We are all well and we hope that you are the same. We are sending you a package of your clothes. We included two new dresses which we hope you will like. Write us as soon as you receive the package.

When do you intend to come home dear daughter? After all who is left here with us. Betty and Minna are married. Every Friday night when I bench [light] the candles I remind myself of the flowers that you used to bring. Papa too misses you. We talk and think about you day and night.

If you surprise us and marry there and come home with a husband I will be glad too.

Lily called and told me that you wrote her. Why don't you write to me more. I love your letters. I feel as though I am reading a good book.

You received a phone call from Camp Sussex asking you to come to camp this summer. The man was very sorry that you couldn't come.

Don't forget to write more often.

Joanie is always asking for you.

Love from Papa and the family.

Your loving
Mother

Regards to the Strod family.

Betty to Celia, Saturday May 2, 1931

My dear Celia,

To begin with, I want to thank you so much for the pretty things you sent to us. The dress for Joanie is too sweet for words. It is exactly her size. Of course she hasn't worn it yet as it is too cold yet, but just as soon as it is warm enough, she is going to display it in the neighborhood. It will indeed cause a great deal of comment, you may be sure, as everyone's business is everybody else's business around here and yours especially seems to worry the neighbors as they keep continually asking for you.

The doll delighted Joanie and the Arab robes caused a riot here. Papa put a Turkish towel on his head one Sunday afternoon and donned the blue robe and walked downstairs into the store. The usual Sunday guests were there and he had them all in stitches. He did look very funny. His face has a sort of pallor and the contrast of the blue and silver against it made him look like a real Arab. You can imagine the uproar. Yidis Brick just couldn't stop laughing. She almost had an accident! That's that.

Lillian looks wonderful. Believe me, if you have half her color you must be getting good looking. Be careful, or one of those Arabian sheikhs will fall for you. There must be some very handsome men out in Palestine, as I once had an Arabian Jewish boy friend and he was wonderful.

There is really not much news to write about.

Without a doubt Lily wrote you of the passing of our dear uncle Borich Yusel. It was all so sudden. I saw him the night before he died. He did not look so well, but I never dreamt he would go so quickly. It was a heart attack. We all deeply grieve for him. He was such a fine person. "May his soul rest in peace."

Annie asked to be remembered to you. She has also become a business woman. Her husband bought a fruit store and so she has to be the salesgirl.

Minna has already furnished her home. It is a very cozy place. She thinks married life is great and she is more in love than ever. Her husband is very aloof. He seldom comes here. Mama is the one who takes this marriage more to heart than anyone else. It is really making her sick. Last week she was so ill, she really almost died. She is feeling better again now. Papa sent her to Lakewood for two weeks, but the climate did not agree with her and she came back feeling worse than when she left. I have an idea that if she took a trip to Jerusalem and stayed there for six months she would come back in A condition. I am encouraging her to do so. I really think Pop would not mind. What do you think. Write and let her know.

We sent you the package of clothes. I went with Minna and bought you two dresses. One for business and the other to wear when you go out. I hope you'll like them.

I want to take Joanie to the movies so I'm going to finish this letter with best regards from all.

Lots of love
Betty

P.S. I expect to send you Joanie's picture shortly.

Minna to Celia, June 29, 1931

Dear Tzip,

Why haven't we received any mail from you now for more than a month? Lily got a letter from you last week, but Mama feels terrible because you didn't write to her. We sent you a white coat with some girls that left about 2 weeks ago. Also, did you receive the package of clothes we sent.

The family is O.K. But Mama is not so well. In fact she's been sick all along. And you know how she worries when you don't write to her. She thinks you just went away, never to come home.

By the way, when do you intend to return. Mama and Papa wanted to cable to you when you didn't write. After all, there is hardly anyone with them and they feel that you don't care for them at all and a letter certainly helps to cheer them up.

Papa looks old already and Mama is not getting younger either. I hate to write you all this, but it's just how things are, here. Mama is hardly able to stay in the store and her asthma has made her very weak and she worries when she doesn't hear from you.

I want to tell you about little Joany. She's some kid. She talks about you and says she misses you. Betty bought her a little violin and she's taking lessons. She's learning, too. Imagine her, a kid at three with her little violin. She's adorable.

Mama says, if you're angry because of the $50 that Papa has, you needn't worry because it's always here for you.

I'm sorry to tell you that our beloved Uncle Motel passed away about five weeks ago. He had been ill all along and one day he was out riding with his son Benny. He got a heart attack and died in Benny's arms. The folks took it pretty badly. Celia please write to Mama.

Best regards
Your loving sister
Minna

Picture postcard from Palestine ("Jerusalem: Dormition of the Virgin on Mount Sion"), Celia to Mr. and Mrs. A. Antopolsky, July 23, 1931

Mother & Father, and dear all-of-you,

I've already sent a cable just to tell you I am well. I've received the dresses and the coat and Minna's letter; and I am heart-broken about Uncle Motel's death. I shall write more very soon. My deep love to you all,

Celia

The clothes are charming. Thank you much and much.

Minna to Celia, Monday, August 16, 1931

Dear Celia,

Well, at last we have your letter and Mama and Papa rejoiced to hear from you. But they miss you. They say it's a year since you've gone and that you don't seem to want to come home. You can always take a trip back there again if you wish. Papa and Mama feel that something is at the bottom of your desire to stay there. They are getting old, Celia, and they miss you. Irving is in the country and never writes. Betty and Joanie are away too. After all who have they got with them? No one! They feel, Celia, that you just don't care for them. Mama says that if you could possibly come home just for a while. Then you could return again when you wished. She's very anxious to see you again. You know how mothers are. You know somehow now that I'm married and have my own home I'm beginning to realize by sort of looking on from outside, the sort of rotten struggling time of it, that Mama and Papa have. It hurts me terribly and because I have realized it I have grown more and more attached to them. I come here when I can, help them, sympathize—but they're not so happy.

They want to see you. They're confident that you could find a good position here in New York. They want to see you married. I suppose you know how they feel. Think it over, Tzip, and just try to realize how they're taking this whole business of your being away a year from home.

Please write to Mama and Papa and tell them just what you plan.

Love from Mama and Papa and
Minerva

Minna to Celia, September 24, 1931

Dearest Sister Cel,

By this time you shall have received money and a cable from Papa. We received your beautiful letter wishing us a Happy New Year. [The Jewish New Year, September 12, 1931]. Well, Yom Kipper has come and gone. And you will be interested to know that it was ushered in by a son (another one) born to our beloved cousin Carrie. She had a fairly good birth this time—no hemorrhages. Well it's her fourth, thank God, and Aunt Ruchel is delighted.

Now about the money Papa sent: you see, Tzip, we really want you to come home, and papa thought that you want to come home, too, but that you hadn't enough money; therefore, he sent it. So, if you really want to, you can pack up and ankle home. I assure you, you'll get some welcome.

I am taking advantage of an "evening off" by writing to you. My Sweetheart wandered off somewheres with brother Irving, who had dinner with us tonite. I don't expect them back for a while yet so here I am. Irving looks wonderful, Celia. He's a man! He came back from the country with a swell coat of tan and so tall and broad-shouldered. I'm proud of him! He's entered his last year at school now, and he's very very much interested in his law. He also is very popular with the ladies this year.

Betty looks about the same. A trifle plumper, perhaps, but still the same sweet (?) thing.

Joanie is perfectly adorable. You won't know her. She talks like a grownup and is the apple of Mama and Papa's eyes.

As for the new, married Minna, I assure you that she doesn't look married. She has changed in her mind, perhaps, has a deeper sympathy for people, a finer outlook on life, more of an understanding. She is no longer the rotten, mean kid sister you had. She has changed—And all because of the fulfillment of a beautiful Love—

I was just interrupted. They delivered our radio. We have the cutest little apartment. And by the way Mama has a radio too.

Mama is still suffering from that darned Asthma, but she is still the sweetest Mother in the world. Papa is just about the same. He is painting the entire house. He wants you to come home. How about it? Write. Al sends his love. So does the whole family and Mother and Papa.

Lovingly,
Minna

Chapter 23

"Did she fall in love with someone there?"
(Correspondence among Celia Antopolsky, Lillian Shapiro
and Joey Marks, May 4, 1931 to August 26, 1931)

Celia to Lillian and Joey, May 4, 1931

P.S. Enclosed please find me, smiling for a change!

Lillian, Darling and Joey,

I glory in your happiness. I'm glad, glad, glad, Lillie, that you are not going to teach! Joey, dear lad, recognize the fact that my "chaverah" is a princess on earth and there are few like her, and the poor and sick will soon vanish now that Lillian has set to work with such dispatch among them.

I'm delighted, of course, that Ellis is coming. It is surely time that he has his immortal adventure, although I have become so calloused of heart that I may pull away from his fairy tale even as he strove once to pull away from mine. But with-it-all, vain and fickle as I am, I look at you two, and I see what longing has done for Ellis and I know beyond all doubt that the Madison Colony, conceived and executed in the image of an inner beauty, has not lived and died in vain.

I have met _____ and _____ here, but neither of them impresses me greatly. I find myself intolerant of merely "nice" girls. What do I want? Some vengeful fire, some passionate credo, some vivid rebellion? Colour, that is all I seek now, colour in music, and art and life. There, with one gesture of my pencil, I toss a rainbow into your lives, and I shall wait with you, dear ones, until the colours die, and night draws its hood, and sets up the stars for light.

Lillian, many people send you good wishes. Marcus, Emma and Louis, Mayor, Ginsberg, Grossman, Miss Silver of the American Express, Dr. Fishel, many others.

I am trying now to get a permanent visa for a year through the influence of Beck indirectly and the Municipal Government directly. This does not mean that I will necessarily stay for a year but it will do away with the difficulty of constant renewals. Meanwhile, I still love life here and hate the thought of returning to New York. Our special attractions at the moment are glorious spring days, one after the other, and white, moon-filled nights.

Lillian, dear, you must draw on my fifty dollars, if my father still has it, and I commission you to send me by way of Ellis, the following: (size 18 will do. I have become thinner, praise be the gods!) listed according to importance!

<u>Woolworth accessories</u>

1 white summer coat, which I simply must have as I am left entirely without a spring coat, as you know, and the evenings are cool.

1 white sport dress, with a blue or green jacket if possible.

1 long dress, chiffon perhaps, in a good color for me.

A couple of pairs of silk stockings

Some decent underwear.

Lillian, do <u>not</u> buy the major items if you cannot get the money from my father. If you can, however, you might shop with Minna who would be pleased, I know, if you asked her to help you choose things.

I have received a beautiful letter from her and Al and I really feel that there is no great tragedy in their marriage. After all Bunny Seal [Celia and Lillian's landlady in Jerusalem] is married to an Englishman and I am in a position to see how happily they live together.

I feel terribly sorry about my letter to Harry Neiman. He has returned it with a proud, rather hurt, note and I have already written to justify myself. I had completely forgotten the contents of the letter, and the ridiculous mood that possessed me at the moment of writing. In any case, I have put in a new claim to be forgiven.

Write to me, dear-both-of-you. I want to hear the details of the respective jobs.

I am seriously considering Joey's proposal and will try to whip my brain-children into a semblance of decency for publication.

I leave you now, but I shall come again soon.

Lovingly,
Celia

Lillian to Celia, on memorandum form, "May 14, 1931, In the office," enclosing a Proof of Claim from the Bank of the United States

Dear C,

Sign the enclosed Proof of Claim and return it <u>immediately</u> to me. I will turn it in at the bank.

Perhaps, maybe, efsher [Hebrew for "perhaps"]—money may be forthcoming.

Pater, your mother told me, called your house for your Palestinian address. Perhaps he has a prick of conscience.

Your family, yesterday, were discussing a Palestinian trip in the good old California type of discussion. Irving has the idea of going just for the summer—getting a job as musician on the boat.

Your family may not go, but their discussions are of sufficient heat to give them a sense of accomplishment.

Love,
Lillian

Write, won't you?

Lillian to Celia, May 28, 1931

> Waiting, while two of my clients' children are being given vocational guidance tests, psychological tests and other methods man has devised of attempting to define what he knows nothing about. But, of course, we use electricity without knowing its composition.

Celia, dear,

Do you mind if I was amused by the last letter I received from you? it sounded like a kindly aunt writing with an eye for having the letter read by the family, saying "God bless you, my children." Don't try joint letters. I don't think they are successful, because letters should be personal, i.e. from one person to another—not to two. The temptation is great, however, to kill two birds with one stone—I have just done the same thing myself; written a joint letter to the Palestinian girl and the boy who took me around Paris. It is not successful.

Last night, I saw the finest, most complete play of the season, "The Barretts of Wimpole Street," with Katharine Cornell. It is the story of Elizabeth Barrett and Robert Browning. Each character fitted his part perfectly, down to the minor characters. Robert Browning is represented as charming, tall, strong boyish face, full of vitality. Mr. Barrett presents an interesting psychological case.

I also saw *S. S. Pinafore*, still with Fay Templeton in the role of Buttercup. Gilbert & Sullivan still draw a full house in New York—and there are no misplaced laughs.

This is the first evening I am home in ages. My mother, in her usual sweet manner, does not wish to be honored with my presence at meals. Even being at home, I am very detached. I am hardly affected by what does or does not happen in this house.

Joey has been placed in charge of the New York policies for his firm. They think he is much older than he is and he has been entrusted with a great deal of responsibility—he is doing the work of three men who were dismissed after being in the organization for many years. Last week, for instance, a new bookshop opened in the Empire State Bldg. Joey was there when they were fumbling with the setting-out of the windows. He got into the window, and within a half hour, set up a very attractive display of the autobiography of Al Smith (pub. by Doubleday Doran), with original tin-types of his youth, etc. Al Smith sent word he was pleased with it and is sending Joey an autographed copy of the book.

Yesterday Joey set out another window for them (he enjoys doing it). I saw it tonight and it is most attractive and in very good taste.

Continued June 3, 1931

Dearest Chaverah,

(Note in passing: the first part of my letter was so factual because my mother was delivering one of her Gettysburg addresses, and although it means nothing to me, it interferes with connected thought. I am grateful that now that we are no longer on speaking terms, I must answer to no-one for my actions).

I just received your letter mailed May 20th, and you have no idea of the happiness it brings me. First: because you are happy. Celia, I feel as if you have been through a baptism which has left you clean of pettiness and artificiality. How few people have the sense of truth and courage to achieve it! I do not condemn, but I pity the others.

For your own sake, I am happy at your reaction to the Ellis situation. I did not wish to mention it further or offer opinions until I received your reaction—and I am glad for you. And I am really to some extent sorry for Lee. I have been to their place several times. She is sincere, has good in-telligence, is very much in love with Ellis, I believe; and she is getting very little satisfaction from a relationship which requires all and gives nothing. Ellis has certainly not overworked himself this year; Lee works during the day and prepares evening meals.

Last Sunday a week ago, Joey called Ellis because he had to return something borrowed from Ellis. Lee answered the phone. It was 4 p.m.

181

She was beginning the preparation of dinner. She expected him soon. We arrived at 6:30 p.m. Lee was still waiting for Ellis. He was at a Brooklyn Young Judaea field day. He came in at 7 p.m., somewhat tired. Lee cheerfully set the table, served the food for both, washed and wiped the dishes. Ellis did nothing but eat, rest, and talk. When Lee was thru, she suggested a cinema. She waited indoors all afternoon and wanted to go out for a bit. Ellis with his usual bored air did not wish to stir.

Ellis is leaving on his glorious adventure. What will Lee have? Certainly not an overdose of friends, because most people regard her as married.

Ellis is charming, and enthusiastic about Palestine and you—but I hope you won't be swept away by it. I wish it were otherwise, but Ellis is not the "giving" type—that is all.

From your description, I can close my eyes and breathe in Jerusalem—how much it means to the "initiated."

The clock says 1:40 A.M. now and tomorrow morning I must take two intelligent children of unintelligent parents to Aquarium, Battery Park, etc.

I shall get you the coat if possible. I already have some Woolworth's odds and ends to send, but I am waiting to collect all together.

Your folks are well, Joany speaks of you continually (your letters meant a great deal to your mother. They cheer up the family)—and I, 30 years from now, will be heir to $5,000. My grandfather left a provision whereby Harold and I receive $5,000 at the death of my grandmother.

Lots and lots of love from Joey and Lillian

Lillian to Celia, June 23, 1931

Dearest Celia,

Have you stopped dreaming, since you write of no suffering? To think that Celia Antopolsky is now an indispensable secretary! Dr. Kenworthy, with whom I am taking a course in social work psychiatry at the N.Y. School for Social Work, would call it an excellent adjustment to your environment.

However, couldn't you be that little bit unadjusted so that you would have to reach the balance by writing? If you could only send some things, poetry or stories, enough for a small volume, Joey could have it read by the editor of Doubleday Doran and accepted if they think it marketable.

As soon as I read your letter, I telephoned your mother. She has been worried, despite my assurances, because you have not written her for a month. She feasts on every word you send her when you do send it. The Minnie situation caused her a good deal of heart-ache as soon as neighbors began questioning—"I understand that your daughter married an Italian?"

Do write to her! It means so much to her happiness.

Well, Ellis has finally left after a great many insipid Young Judaea parties—given by the city, the national organization, the Brooklyn leaders, the Brooklyn children etc., their only virtue being that each gathering presented Ellis with a gift. At one of them, there were speeches made about these "pioneer" Young Judaeans pointing the way for others to follow. Each of the recipients made speeches thanking the donors and telling of their expectations. Only Joshua Trachtenberg was honest. He said "Thanks for the gift. But about the business of idealism—we are fooling ourselves if we think we are going as <u>chalutzim</u> [pioneers]. We are not. We are going to see the country and have as good a time as we know how!"

However, the sailing of the Europa was impressive. From the pier, Young Judaean leaders sang their Palestinian songs with spirit (many on the boat including Weisgal were going to the Congress), and at 12:30 midnight, two little tugs smoothly pulled the immense ship out of the dockspace, and into the harbor.

Ellis is returning with the camera—as our agreement specified. If you get any good views, won't you send me copies?

Celia, if you can, don't lose your head when Ellis comes—I say this because I want you to be happy. His lack of accomplishment and lack of frankness is sensed by his old friends.

For once, let your head as well as your heart decide. Whatever your decision—let the gods be with you. Of course, as usual, I place full faith in you to keep these confidences .

I am taking your statement of being "alone" with as much salt as the specific gravity of the Yam Hamelech [the Dead Sea]. Despite your protestations to the contrary, 'tis you who will fall one of these days. It's a feeling in me bones, somewhat like rhumatics but not quite as sharp.

Last week, I went out with Joe R___. Give his regards to his sister. I hurt him very much when I decided not to accept his next invitation—he is one of those "too insistent" men.

It is late, and tomorrow is a work-day. Yes! I shall work throughout the summer.

Lots & lots of love to you.

June 25, 1931

I intended ending the letter here, but it didn't get mailed. Therefore the continuation.

Have you noticed my jerky style? That comes of dictating concise casework records.

Yesterday I stopped in at Girls Commercial [High School] to have our licences signed for filing. This is the first time I have seen Mrs. Allen [the Principal] since I am back. She was very much interested in what you were doing in Palestine (she asked the same question almost everyone asks when they discover that you stayed on, "Did she fall in love with someone there?") and in my work here.

My best regards to everyone in the city of stones. Let them not think too harshly of me for not writing, because—well, you remember New York if you can think that far back in your life.

I must close now, for in five minutes I have an appointment with another one of these men in whom hope springs eternal—I try not to be too hard on them, except when they are like Joe R____.

So once again, lots of love to you from

Lillian

Joey and Harold both send love, as well as Aaron.

How is your Hebrew progressing? Do you see Njura at all?

Joey saw a notice in the publisher's weekly that Pater is publishing a book of contemporary poetry called "Symphonies." Joey is trying to get his address. I understand Pater called your home for your address. Have you heard from him? I should be interested in seeing whether he put any of your poetry in it.

Letter from Alan Frederick Pater, typed on letterhead of "Literary Publications, 580 Fifth Avenue, Suite 1010, New York City" dated July 25, 1930

Sevia:

I, too, have gone on a vacation; your letter to me, was forwarded to my address here in the country where I am staying. I was glad to receive it.

There is scarcely anything of importance I can think of to write to you. You see, business has virtually flitted from my mind. To write of the beauty of this place, would be telling you so much of what you already know. I am quite at a loss of what to write to you.

Although I do miss some of your verse. Have you written anything new? If so, what? Will you send me some? Please do. You may send your next letter, if it is not too long in arriving to the address I have put on the bottom of this letter. Please do write.

Most sincerely,

(Signed) Pater

PATER

ALAN PATER

KAPLAN'S MONGAUP HOUSE

Box 134

Hurleyville, New York.

Luzon Station, Sullivan County

Letter from a former student of Celia's, Tel-Aviv, August 5, 1931

Dear beautiful Miss Celia Antopolsky,

I was very glad to see you in our house in Tel-Aviv. You are very good, you are always so jolly that you took my heart in prison.

At the beginning I stood bashful for you, but at last I liked you very much. I think you whould (sic) not be angry with me, that I did not write to you until now. I had no Time to write. The tests came along one after another so that I was very busy.

I beg you to exuse (sic) me.

Your sincerely
Tova-Dafna

My address:
Tova-Dafna
Eliaser ben-jehuda 33
Tel-Aviv, Palestine

Send me your picture, pleas (sic).

Celia to Lillian, begun August 26, 1931, and not completed or sent

My beloved Chavera—

I have been storing things, like an ant, to tell you. Yet the days here have a way of slipping by so that the wish never meets the act, and my letter is unwritten and unwritten, until suddenly I become panicky, grit my teeth, grasp a pen, and, at midnight, start at the very beginning.

There's my job. The El Wad Sewer Reconstruction has finally come to an end after Mr. Beck, working on a 10% commission basis, spent twice as much money as the city had planned for, incidentally money derived from Jewish taxation. These many months have taught me to know Beck very well and he has come to be very small in my eyes. While we are on very good terms, I find that I have no respect for him. He is unspeakably selfish, grasping, and mean. He wishes people to give their whole thoughts and to dedicate their very lives to the furtherance of his ambition. Besides, while Jews have been the brains of his organization, he shows in a thousand ways his hatred for them. His social life is almost entirely with Arabs, since he is trying to capture the good favour of the municipal government, which is hopelessly rotten. As far as my relationship to him is concerned, of course, until now I was at El Wad and I was really fascinated by the job there. The glamour of the Old City, the Arab house, the infinite problems of the work made my days keen and swift-flying. I timed my work actually by the call of the muezzins coming high and clear twice a day from the neighboring mosques.

But on the 31st of August, my work for the municipality ends. Now, Beck wants to retain me as his Private Secretary. He is beginning again now, in a sense; hunting for a new job and not prepared to spend one additional mil until he gets one. Of course, I struck for regular hours and a salary of at least LP20. We compromised on LP12 for September with an increase to LP20 if we secured any one of the various jobs for which he is tendering, the increase to be retroactive for the month of September. We are now in his private office; you remember it, dim and overstuffed with furniture. It would be pleasant enough for one person, but it now contains a draughtsman's table, the Chief Accountant's desk, Mr. Beck's desk, and my typewriter table, and four of us are working at each other's elbows. I am not happy in it. The necessary routine work now does not interest me. I have the unpleasant opportunity of seeing all Mr. Beck's petty scheming, his bickering in all of his dealings with people, and I must listen to his endless account of feats he has accomplished and the greatness he looks for in the future. Were he a fine man, I should be eager to help him now, but, since he is what he is, I hate to think of furthering his interests as against Jewish interests, though he does not hesitate to use Jews for his own ends. So much for my job.

If I had some money, I should leave it. Since I have none, I shall probably carry on for a while, but not for long. I want a new adventure!

The Young Judaeans have come to town. [letter breaks off here]

Staff of the El Wad Sewer Project

Chapter 24

Languidly, I think of going back

(Correspondence between Harry Neiman and Celia Antopolsky,
June 23, 1931 to November 16, 1931)

Harry to Celia, June 23, 1931

Dear Celia,

I know little about the climate in J but it is very hard to think of any place that is more uncomfortable than NY at present. The heat is so great, or should I say the humidity, that even I, ambitious and industrious person that I am, think nothing of leaving the office each afternoon at 1 p.m. and going for a dip. The finest things extant in this part of the world just now are the ocean, ices, lemonades etc. for the sun beats down even more fiercely than is usual even with Him, or is the Sun a she, and what with unemployment, decreased business etc. we are, most of us, reduced to misery.

There is one cheering thing, however. Herbie Hoover, Cal Coolidge, Andy Mellon, Lamont et al issue daily statements telling the world (Americans in particular because they are the most gullible and because election time is drawing near) that the dark days are almost gone; that soon, very soon, we will turn the corner and meet Prosperity, that shy Miss with the exaggerated sense of humor who would make us believe that there was something wrong with us and that she had left us, while in truth and in fact, she was only taking shelter, temporarily, because she did not want to be hit by falling stocks. Now that the storm has spent itself she (Prosperity) like the brave little standby that she is (created 'specially for

Americans and the Republican Party by a politically minded God) would, and will, come and lift up and patch up the wounded and place them on their feet again. From this can be deduced that there's nothing wrong with the system here. The cause of the trouble is that the stocks went down and down and business all over the country went to pot. Leave it to nurse Prosperity, she'll fix everything! And by the way, don't forget to vote for Hoover, he's got an in with Miss Pros, she who used to be Cal Coolidge's best girl.

What I really ought to tell you is that last week after trying a case at 264 Madison Street I suddenly decided to walk over and look over the old dump you used to stay in at #400; then when I got to 397 I saw a sign reading, "Just renovated, 3 room apts, elec etc., reasonable, inquire Janitor." I did, was shown a really bright cheerful kitchen, bedroom and living room on the second floor; another on the 4th that was even brighter and more cheerful; asked for the price and was told that it was $15; offered $10, closed the deal at $12 per month and became the owner of an apartment on a fashionable street like Madison St.

If you continue to stay away your people are sure to disown you and you ought to be bolstered by the feeling that if worse comes to worse there is always a home? waiting for you on good, old, smelly Madison St. with the candy store and telephone just across the street.

The honest truth is, of course, that I want to throw a few little parties that are a little beyond the pale of respectability and need just such a "hide-out." The good feature about this house is that there are no families of women and children on the stoop eyeing you wonderingly and suspiciously as you come and go; the house is occupied by young men and women keeping bachelor apartments.

There is on East Broadway, nearby, a very powerful Democratic Club, the Ahearn Democratic Club, of which I am to become a member at their next meeting, Tuesday. In this way I will meet all the Municipal Court Judges as they rotate through the court on Madison St., where I now bring all my cases. I am also going to make 397 Mad. St. my voting address.

Perhaps, at this rate, it will be I who will hand you the keys to the city when you get home (by the way, you monkey, when are you coming home?) to tell us of your adventures.

Seriously, now. Yesterday, Marcus and Singer & Son, late officials of the Bank of the U.S., were convicted by a jury, after a 12 week trial, of the charge of misapplying the bank's funds, and were sentenced by Judge Donellan to from 3 to 6 years in jail for Marcus and the elder Singer, while the younger Singer, 23, erstwhile clerk in the office of Isidore Knesel, attorney for the bank, and the brains, it is said, of the fraudulent deal, was sentenced to an indeterminate term—this means he will serve no more than 3 years in jail. Rich, powerful, respected in the banking world only yesterday, today broke, jeered at and hissed by exultant crowds, they walk over the Bridge of Sighs to the Tombs, forever disgraced, convicts. They, as bankers; my father, as a realtor; countless hundreds of thousands in their businesses, large and small, were victims of that universal disease "get rich—quick." Each saw in himself a Napoleon in his field. Marcus and Singer visioned themselves Morgans and Rothschilds; my father, a Jacob Astor; a little tailor, president of the National Cloak & Suit Company—easy bank credits, overexpansion—calling in of loans—crash.

Perhaps I should have gone to the movies after all. Has Charlie Chaplin in City Lights come to Palestine yet? Are there moving pictures in Palestine? Are there any other foolish questions I can ask you?

Can you let me have some more paper? It is only 12:30 AM and there's some ink left in this pen.

Sweet, you must write me more about yourself. Nothing is too trivial or uninteresting. How you managed to get your jobs, what your duties are, the sort of men you worked for and with, what you do for relaxation and diversion, whether you are doing any writing—any thing and everything about yourself.

Forgive all the nonsense in this letter, Sweet, but tonight I feel so light and gay and glad, that somehow my pen seems to glide, literally, over the paper, albeit irregularly, and the words, jumbled, undignified, thoughtless, come faster than usual, and were I not out of writing paper or faced with the necessity of rising early tomorrow and going to Snyder Ave. Brooklyn to try some boring auto accident case, I would scribble and ramble on indefinitely. Luckily for you, I must now say, good night, Celia, keep well and let me hear from you soon and often.

Harry

Celia to Harry, July 7, 1931, typed in the office

Dear Soon-to-be-great Lawyer-man, Harry,

Are not the administration of justice, yea, with an honest soul, and the salving of consciences that hurt, difficult and arduous tasks in the middle of the summer? Does not your soul pant (like the hart) after cool spaces and running waters? Let this letter be to you as a wind from the hills and may it pass, like a white hand of peace, over your head, and may you be refreshed and removed for a moment from the deep-seated wickedness of men.

Dear Harry, your letter was a brave one indeed, because I don't deserve to be considered so gently, nor so generously forgiven for my impulses which, although well-meant, are altogether too heedless and hurt too often for me to go unpunished as I do. Now, we are friends again, and I can tumble my irresistible (in the sense that I cannot resist using them) words over the paper for your especial benefit, and know that you won't take them too seriously, and that you will realize that my thoughts grow in my head like weeds and should be pulled out more often than not.

You ask what holds me in Jerusalem. Friends, for I have made many, the peace of the hills which I have never before found anywhere, the sweet, cool nights in midsummer, my work that still fascinates me, and a dread of the heat and noise and grime of tawdry New York. That's all, but more than enough to make me a willing stranger in the gates. More than enough to make me drift with time through the year, and not care when I shall suddenly decide to return to those who are still held rooted even against their will.

Some day, dear ambitious lad, you will have your freedom, too, and then perhaps you will come to see for yourself that there are other things than the necessity for artificial diversion, which makes it a crime not to go out on Saturday night, other things than the mad need for money which beats down the best years of one's life; yea, even in a garden there are those here who have found their souls. And I know how all that's fine in you, Harry, struggles now that eventually you may have the leisure to examine beauty at will, and because of this, I wish you a heaping measure of the world's success and the clear vision to evaluate it exactly for its worth.

And have I preached too much? I did not mean to. I wished only to speak to you as if it were twilight on the earth and the time for softly-spoken confidences had come, and my voice was softer than the whisper of a breeze, and you wanted to listen though it didn't matter much what was said.

Write to me soon, and would you 'phone my mother that all is well with me?

Celia

Harry to Celia, begun July 4, 1931, continued July 27, 1931

Dear Celia,

Today I met a fellow to whom you introduced me last year in the library; his name is Wortman. Remember him? He did not recognize me but his appearance and general air is of such a wistful sort that I refreshed his recollection as to who I was. Of course, he spoke about you, mostly, very interested in Palestine, naturally, and with a very genuine enthusiasm told me that next July, one year hence, he, too, was going to Palestine. I learned that he was serving a clerkship in a law office; that he was soon to be admitted to the profession; that soon he was to become a citizen of the U.S.; that he was writing something or other etc. etc. And now, most important, he wants you to find out whether an attorney can make money, rather a living, in Palestine. Apparently he would settle down there if that were the case. He suggested that I should relay the info to him when you had completed an exhaustive investigation of legal opportunities. I countered with the suggestion that he write you himself; that I knew how delighted you would be to hear from him. He has your address now. Am I forgiven?

The 100% Americans are making this an old fashioned 4th. Even now at 1 a.m. the fireworks are going full blast.

Have you heard that a certain German, Schmelling by name, a prize fighter, had the bad taste to paste, sock, wallop, lambast and knock out an American prize fighter, Stribling by name, a fine upstanding 100% American from below the Mason and Dixon line? You should have seen the faces of those patriots who, hearing the news over the radio in the street, muttered, "Them lousy Germans."

July 27, 1931

I had expected a letter from you daily so that I held this until your letter finally did come and I resume now.

Last week, just after reading your letter, I 'phoned home and spoke to your father and delivered your message. He was, of course, glad to hear from you, but oh, so disappointed that you did not send it more directly. Then he asked me when you were coming home and there, unfortunately, I was unable to give the slightest satisfaction. Altogether the conversation was unsatisfactory, I think, even though I did speak my best Yiddish and had sufficiently identified myself to your father so that he said, Oh, Harry from New York, I know you.

How impressive the City Engineer's stationery is and how busy you must be to type your letters to me!

I did not think you preached and even if you did it was necessary to get your point over—which you did. Yet Celia, you do have friends in America, too and New York isn't all hot and tawdry, you know; and your friends here are not of the ones who think it a crime not to go out of a Sat. night. Have you forgotten us altogether, Celia?

Last week, I mean two weeks ago, I spent an evening with Lillian (Marks absent, too) and we talked and talked and talked, mentioned you once or twice, too. I had especially wanted to do that so as to understand you the better in relation to Palestine. All the more so because Wortman had said to me, "I can understand why Celia remains there, even though her friend left and even if her family wants her home, for I know that the love one has for Palestine is greater than the love one has for parents." I confess that I thought the remark a stupid and thoughtless one at the time, and still do, yet after talking to Lillian, I can understand that it holds more for you than Brooklyn does. Yet if you're not in love with someone in Palestine, (I wouldn't be surprised if you were), I expect you to come home, not to Brooklyn, not to hot, tawdry, Sat.-night-pleasure-seeking New York, but to the New York you really do know and like, the New York that has its beautiful spots and memories; to your family and friends who love you differently and better than the like and admiration of those in Palestine.

But I guess all this is a little more than I should have said or a little more than the truth. You probably do admit, do know all the above and yet the kind of life you now lead may mean more to you than family ties and other ties, if you still remember, or have any to remember.

Excuse, please, my extreme seriousness about this matter which after all boils down to this: if you are happy there, happier than you have been here or expect to be here, you should stay in Palestine in spite of all pressure brought upon you to return. Unless, of course, you see your way clear to be able to come here for a short while and return.

And Celia, you must have a host of people who demand to hear from you and your time, I guess, must be very much taken up writing to them—

too much time, if I'm not mistaken. Does that account for the complaint of your family that you seldom write? Dear Celia, suppose, then, you do not feel in the future that you have a letter to answer to Harry Neiman. Only when you have lots of time and do not have to deprive yourself of an interesting time somewhere, I wish you'd write to me. Little monkey, you understand, don't you, what your letters mean to me, but I, too, understand how hard it is for you to please everybody waiting to hear from you.

Love,
Harry

Celia to Harry, August 12, 1931, typed

In the noonday heat of Jerusalem, when scarcely a leaf stirs, and the sun beats down like silent golden thunder

Harry, my dear, dear boy,

Your last long, wide letter filled my heart for many days, but in the pressure of many Americans arriving in Jerusalem, and my services as guide and entertainer being continually called upon, I have been answering your letter all the time theoretically, but not actually, until this moment. That's a funny sentence, isn't it? But that's the way sentences roll off typewriters, each word like a bouncing ball, with no dignity and no individuality. Yet, if I did not utilize this odd moment, you'd never be getting a letter from me, and maybe it wouldn't matter, but maybe it would! Does it still matter?

I still love Jerusalem, but I must honestly confess that the urge of big cities is creeping slowly back into me, and if I weren't such a pauper, I'd be going to Europe now, and then, perhaps, be returning to see the Empire State Building, and hate the subway, and take notes of the imminent success of one Harry Neiman, proud lawyer-lad who may be foolish enough to still want me for a friend.

I was delighted and charmed to hear of your apartment on Madison Street. How I'd have loved helping you with it! And that makes me think, Boy dear, that you haven't had a vacation this summer. I wish you could come with me to cool woods and think of nothing for a whole day, and then another, and watch the sun sift through a million green leaves. But then, I was ever a distraction, and a parasite on the useful members of society, and if it weren't for the knowledge that I bring a bit of natural joy to wherever I stop, I might be sadly conscience-stricken.

My life here goes on simply. New people come and go. The days are eternally gold and blue and dust-grey. Languidly, I think of going back to New York for a while. I cannot think of living there forever any more. But since my return ticket went with the U.S. Bank, I have no money, and the easiest thing to do is to stay on unless I borrow, and I hate to do that because I have no prospect of work when I return. Perhaps you can use me as a secretary. I'm very intelligent and disgustingly efficient and, as one man in my office has just discovered, painfully business-like. What shall I do, Harry? Is it worthwhile coming back now?

I wonder what you are like now. Have you grown much older in this harried year? You never sent that picture and I wonder that you expect me to remember you. I do love to receive your letters. Won't you write soon and much, and give me the advice of excellent counsel. Enough to say that my wanderlust is returning, and I feel that I must try my wings soon, and I may, after all, be flying your way, if the doors of your house are not yet shut.

In the last few weeks, you have come back to me vividly. I don't know why, except that your letter is so full of planning, and eagerness, and joie de vivre, and I love that in people, and I have met too many who are blasé and dulled-with-living-every-day, and they seem to take from me the sparkle of my keenness and give so little in return because, you see, they have nothing to give. That hurts, sometimes. Only there are always the few, few others, and they make it worth while. Like you.

> You will write soon, yes? And you will
> call my mother, dear one man I can
> trust, and I am still, joyously, your
>
> Celia

Harry to Celia, August 26, 1931

> (If Mahomet did it why can't I?
> Ages since I heard from you)

Dear Celia,

The next best thing to receiving letters from you is to write them to you—and so here I am again; very selfish of me, I think, to indulge so much.

I never really understood how prosaic an existence I do lead, until I attempted to write to you what goes to fill the months for me here in New York, and then only did it come to me that while I do keep busy and time almost actually flies, setting the events down honestly on paper makes a very dull resume—especially for one who is so very prejudiced against New York and New Yorkers. And so at a loss to interest you, the best I can hope for is to amuse you. And to do that, don't you think it would be more effectual to write you what goes on inside me than what goes on about me? Or would you prefer not only to be amused but to laugh right out loud and hear what I think of and what I do?

Well, firstly, primarily I think of you—try to remember what you look like, try, with the help of a very willing imagination to bring you very close to me (so close, I'm afraid you'd disapprove—or am I wrong?) and so to walk and talk again as we've walked and talked in what I privately call "the good old days." So much for my inmost thoughts.

And what do I do?

Well, firstly and primarily, I search until I find a slim girl of 23 or

24, with a fuzzy blond mop of hair spread almost fan-shaped over a head with plenty of forehead and back to it. Then, if her eyes are blue and her mouth quick to smile in a certain magnetic (for me) way, I say, "May I talk with you? May I call you Celia? Come with me to Central Park and here's a book of Robert Frost's Poems I want you to read to me. Will you come to Caruso's with me and eat macaroni while I eat spaghetti?" and when the girl answers all these questions agreeably and carries through in the approved manner, I usually am awakened by the alarm clock.

Are we discouraged? No—well, maybe.

Let me tell you about "The Club." You know I am now a member of the Ahearn Democratic Association, whose clubhouse on E. Broadway you may or may not have noticed. At any rate, Eddie Ahearn, former stable-boy, horse-car driver and man about town is its paternal head and my chief. It is considered an honor indeed for one to be selected by him as orderly. The duties of an orderly consist of getting the big boss a glass of water, buying him cigars, etc. Of course, I do not boast that my advancement has been rapid enough to land me that job, but with fair luck I may yet be lackey to the "great" man himself, for only yesterday the big boy said to me—"Tell Gillis (the fellow whose job I covet) to get me a coupla Eskimo pies." Do you see now that the goal is only one step up? One of these days I'll pretend not to be able to find Gillis (how I hate that man) and buy the sweets myself. Perhaps the great man will note that I can handle the difficult assignments on my own. When he does, anything may happen. Didn't I tell you I'll go high someday?

Seriously, though, someday after a particularly pleasant turn of events, such as a sweeping victory on Election Day, I'll really tell the big bum that I've a hankering to serve "the people" in the District Attorney's office. And if I get such a job in a year or two, with a private practice on the side to add to a $3,500 starting salary, I'll be ready to sit back and say—I've arrived—and continue to dream of someday going far away and seeing geographical dots for myself. The future, I tell you, is bright, but the present is a little dark, and often it is a question whether I am on that road that leads to the light. How futile the foregoing, how sad. Yet I remember (may I?) that even in dark places one can be happy if in pleasant company. Tell me it's not all imagination on my part, please. On second thought, don't answer that question. See how cowardly I've become since you went away?

1.30 a.m. good-night

Thursday, Aug. 27th, 1931
12.30 a.m.

Sweet, I just got home—spent the evening at the Club and had a long, weary, sweaty ride home in the subways we're all so proud of. Mother has been feeling badly about my sleeping overnight at the ap't and so to please her I'll be home as much as possible this week.

I've made the acquaintance tonight of a lawyer who has been a member of the Club for years. Says he to me, "I've been watching you lately, and I can see you're different than these kike lawyers that hang around here. Keep this under your hat. There's gonna be fire-works around here soon. I don't like the way things is being run around here and I think it's 'bout time this outfit had a new leader. Are you with me?" What a startling conversation! What impressed me most is that this man must be either very stupid or very daring. To talk to me, almost a stranger, in this way was to put himself in a position that is precarious indeed. Should I tell Ahearn what he said my ambitious friend would get a swift kick in the pants out of the Club and into Coventry. Daring he is too, for the big boss is as surely enthroned as Stalin and no break in sight. Be that as it may, I'm not committing myself either way, and when and if things do come to a head, and who knows but that they may, I'll jump on the band-wagon like a good politician always does and swear fealty to the powers that be.

Two years ago I'd be ashamed to confess what I do now. But I do want the Ass't District Atty's job.

Goodnight, dear, I'm tired—will finish and mail this letter tomorrow.

Friday Aug. 28/31

Good evening, dear girl, if persistency counts at all, I'll yet finish this M.S.

Celia dear, do we see each other soon? Does it make any difference that I wish it were soon? But of course it doesn't and if I weren't too lazy I'd rewrite this page, leaving out the absurd question.

Take care of yourself, sweet.

Harry

Harry to Celia, September 3, 1931

Dear Celia,

Just after mailing my last letter to you the postman walked in with yours. It was a great surprise. You came closer to me than you have in any letter thus far and, too, you seemed to infer an early departure from Palestine!

I did as you told me—called your home and in answer to the inevitable—"When is she coming home," I answered (you'll be angry at me, I think, but I'd rather have you angry at me in NY than pleased with me from Palestine) "as soon as she gets the money." Whereupon Sister exclaimed, "why only yesterday my father told me to cable her that she must come home and that he'd be glad to send her the money." You probably have received the money by this time. Am I forgiven?

I think it necessary for me to add that nothing would have pleased me more than to have sent you the money myself. I think I understand the reluctance of young people (ahem) to accept aid from the family when "out on their own." I hope you accept quickly and catch the first available ship heading towards U.S.A.

Lillian and Marks came to the office on Saturday. They agreed with me while chewing a steak (rib) at Green's that it would be nice to see you again. Both she and Marks are getting along splendidly at their work and with each other. Lil complains that she's not received a letter from you since June. If that is so you should be ashamed—a little bit, anyhow. She'll not write until she hears from you, she says.

I'm jumpy and irritable tonight and although all this is garbled and scribbled and almost unreadable, I'll send it along just the same and try again in a few days.

Love, dear Celia
Harry

8 or 9 hrs sleep in the last 2 nights and a jury trial to be continued tomorrow. More soon in detail. Excuse this scribble darling.

Harry to Celia, September 30, 1931

Darling,

This much is true: that the days go by quickly, so full and hurried, almost "harried," that I feel cheated every now and then when I look up, figuratively, and notice how quickly the weeks go by. But if they go by quickly, too quickly, I confess I think of you in spite of it all and through it all; and it is always with anticipation that I look through the morning mails for a letter from you with the long looked for announcement of your return. And if the above sounds muddled it is because one, rather I, cannot write with serenity about certain subjects (you). Why the hell don't you come back, you son of a beehive? Do you notice that I cannot, rather will not, understand your reasons for staying away? I'll let you in on a secret: I want you to become so exasperated with my stupidity that you'll come home to explain, with gestures. There, you have my secret and now I guess it'll be years before you come home. You see, I wanted to play fair.

Haven't been feeling well for the last few weeks. The constant wear and tear about the office (how different it is when one has no boss and is intensely interested in every little thing that comes up day by day) have made me nervous and jumpy, so that any delay at a subway station restaurant, anywheres—

even now when I find writing slow and laborious, makes me suffer. I wonder, do you understand what I'm getting at. I do need the vacation that I should have taken (how sweet of you, dear girl, to have noticed that I did not take one this year) and realize now that it was a mistake to think I could save the money and buy the things the family did have real need of. I now look forward to Christmas week when I think I'll go away. I have to smile as I write—no doubt at Christmas I'll be looking forward to something else.

There are thousands of men in NY doing what I am and not letting it get their goats. But I guess being married to a large family and hearing of nothing but rent, rent, rent, bills, bills, bills all the time and just keeping abreast of things no matter how hard you work is a little different than the feeling that if things go well, all right, if not, better luck next time—with me they must go well, must pan out every week and if they don't what is the beloved gang at home going to do?

You see what a coward I am, writing to you, telling you all this—asking you ridiculous questions—

Will write again next week. Will send this off in spite of the jackass it must make me out to be. Punishment, don't you know?

Am going to call Lillian tomorrow, take her to dinner and the movies, ride a 5th Ave. bus and talk talk talk—about you.

Discount all the junk contained herein. I'm not going to reread.

But I would like to have you here—

I'm sitting in my bedroom.

Goodnight—Sweet.

PALESTINE POSTS, TELEGRAPHS & TELEPHONES
TELEGRAM
JERUSALEM 22 OC 31

        TO Celia Antopolsky, Amexco Jerusalem

Cannot sorry.

Harry

ANDREA JACKSON

Harry to Celia, November 16, 1931

Dear Celia,
    Can't we forgive each other for being poor?
    I expect you to write soon.
    I hope you are well.

                                Harry

    You must know that it was as hard for me to answer as I did as it was for you to receive it.
    You know I'd have been happy to help the friend I set so much store by.

Chapter 25

Cable her to meet the boat

(Correspondence between Lillian Shapiro and Celia Antopolsky,
August 27, 1931 to December 5, 1931)

Lillian to Celia, August 27, 1931, Brooklyn, New York

Chaverahti [my friend],

You know how I can procrastinate in letter-writing, but you have far exceeded my record. All jesting aside, I am really becoming worried. The last letter received from you came at the beginning of June. This is the third letter since then, outside of the package, and no word from your end. Somehow, it is not like you.

I suppose you are interested in the fate of your sad $100. The regular plan was that a first payment of 30% would be made in early September. However, there is a plan on foot to reorganize the bank completely. Whenever the money is forthcoming, it will be sent to your present address in Jerusalem, unless you write them to the contrary—because that is the address given by you on the affidavit.

I spent this past Saturday with Joey at the Hashomer Hatzair Camp [a Zionist youth camp]. Those children have the latest in Palestinian dances and songs, and a good deal of the spirit. A large group of parents are really worried at losing their children to Zionism and Palestine, because these children have grown away from their parents. Around a large campfire, all the entertainment and merrymaking took place in Hebrew. We left at 11 p.m. for an invigorating, 5 mile walk to town where

207

we found a charming tourist house to stay over. The Lapsons were also there the same evening. Mrs. Lapson teaches them Palestinian dances.

I close now because I am "offen veg" [on my way].

My best regards to Palestinian friends.

Do write,
Shalom v'brucha [Peace and blessings]
Lillian

Joey to Celia, mailed with Lillian's letter dated August 27 with this note enclosed:

Dear Celia,

If this letter remains in my pocket much longer it will probably fall to pieces—and so I promise another installment soon.

Always,
JM

July 12th, 1931

> A hot dry wind comes down Tapscott Street and the sun bursts into a million multicolored fragments on the corner of the kitchen sink. Lillian's mother is away at the country and with only Lillian home I am received at Shapiro Hall as one of the family—Doesn't this sound like one of your own letters?

Celia, you silly ass (But no, that's not the right way to address your well wishing elder, is it?)

That peculiar feeling which I have towards you makes it possible for me to stand a good deal of your foolishness, puns, jokes and occasional fits of temperament and appetite, but one thing I cannot stand and that is:

"I love you, dear children. My blessing."

You make me feel as if I were a young nephew receiving a blessing from an old maiden, but nevertheles, worldly, aunt. And so I say: Celia, you fool. And I'm justified, aren't I?

Don't forget, Miss Antopolsky, that I once almost did you the honour of almost falling in love with you. I think that this qualifies me to talk to you as an old rejected suitor might—respectfully but still with a dash of intimacy.

News of your happiness in Jerusalem makes me very happy. Much as I would give for even a tiny sight of you, I say stay as long as you are happy.

As for myself, I have never been so happy in my life as I have been since Lily came home. Lily is lovelier than ever and still Lily. My work is coming on splendidly and perhaps in the not so distant future we may find you sitting timidly on the edge of a chair in a luxuriously furnished office with me lolling in a big swivel chair behind a huge glass topped desk and I will say "Alright, Miss Anto—what did you say your name was? Oh yes! Antopolovich. I beg your pardon—Antopolska. Yes I will publish your book. Do you think $1,000 will be enough advance royalties" And you will say "Wow, Mr. Marks, a thousand!! You are so kind."

Seriously however, will you let me have any manuscripts you have hanging around and at least I can have them looked over by either our editors or the editors of Harpers and you will no doubt get some useful criticism. I <u>might even</u> have them published.

Celia, don't you think you are taking somewhat of a chance in the expectation of being able to lavish your affection on an unusually large number of kids which you seem to take for granted will be the result of Lily's and my philandering? There is a new version of the nursery rhyme:

"There was an old woman who lived in a shoe,
She had no children because she knew what to do"

But all this is so sordid.

Celia to Lillian, September 3rd, 1931

Chaverah of mine—

Do you know that I love you very much and think of you so often that it is as if I have written again and again? Even now there is a long letter lying in my room waiting for its conclusion, but I am not there and the mail is going and I cannot let it go without me. I am really missing our companionship and understanding, now more than ever, for, in the midst of all my friends, in the midst of my every moment being monopolized, I find myself quite alone, not unhappily so, but sometimes, wistfully.

My spirit delights with the joy you find with Joey. I give you both an overpowering happiness for the new year, and moments of ecstasy, and warmth, and intellectual keenness, and long varied days of comradeship.

My problem, if anything, has intensified since Ellis has arrived. For months, I had steeled my heart against him yet I could not let the boat come into Jaffa without meeting it. Of course, Josh and Edna and others came with Ellis. They brought a whole atmosphere which I could not tolerate in America. Yet I had to be cordial and accept them, even as we accepted Meyer M_____.

But Ellis—I really did not know what to do with him. I was not actively in love with him—that I knew, but he came with such eagerness that I couldn't hurt him. But our old comradeship, I know now, will never come back, unless there is a miracle. Ellis is still easily bored. He won't go to the movies. He doesn't dance. He sulks. And not loving him, I find it hard to tolerate these things, especially as, with Ellis's coming, all my men friends have fallen off, each certain that this is my lover come to take me home. Actually, Ellis is full of his memory of Lee, whom he does not love, and never will, but whose sportsmanship and convenience he will never really relinquish. He came with an ideal of me, waiting with open arms for him and him alone. When he realized that I knew many men here and that they enjoyed my company, he began to undermine my confidence, to tell me that I was not the same, and so I found myself unhappily forced into a continual companionship in which Ellis constantly enumerated my faults thus making me shut up into myself, and taking from me all the joy in living which has been so much a part of me. Unless there is a change, there will have to be a definite break in the situation, because I see no reason why I should suffer Ellis's impatience, his sulky silences and his accusations. The drastic change from company which was so eager for my conversation and reactions to being taken for granted as if I were a wife of seven years' standing is getting on my nerves rather badly.

The really funny note in the whole affair is that Emma Ehrlich, who was keyed up to foster a true romance, is left in the air, because I am sure she has never see two people act quite like this if, by all outside information and signs, they should be madly in love with each other.

Lillian, darling, I received your package and bless you for it. Everyone here sends his love to you many times. Honestly! And my long letter will tell you all the other things a normal letter should contain. But what is uppermost in my chest is off it now and I know you'll understand and not breathe a word of it.

Love to you, Joey and Harold.

Write! I await your letters like the Meshiach [the Messiah].

Celia to Lillian, October 15, 1931

Evening—Jerusalem

My only and beloved chavera,

I wish I could write you a song of songs, here among the old and friendly hills, and tell you how you have been part of me all this full year, though I have written little to you, and have seemed indifferent in my long silences. Yet every word of you has been a glistening bit of joy in my day and your letters cling in my mind for days afterwards. It has not been you or any other human being who has caused my great reluctance to write. It has been rather an odd estrangement between myself and my pen, as if my pen has known that my thoughts were flying in strange, unaccustomed areas and had no desire to settle anywhere. My serious writings have been rare, indeed. Only now, as if the sharp turn of the year to rain and winter has brought me back to my creative self and partly because Ellis's coming has knocked me out of the self-complacency with which I had been drugging myself, I have become heavy-laden with all sorts of restless desires to write and work at my writing. I am utterly dissatisfied with my work of the year and I feel a new strength now which must evolve into a significant form of beauty.

This letter, you see, is in the nature of a declaration of intention. May it tremble not too uncertainly, this intention, for many days upon my horizon!

My last letter, as you know, was a volcanic eruption of emotion which has since, of course, grown cool and settled. Ellis has already changed a good deal and has become again his old charming self. I almost deplore the fact that he makes so delightful a companion since it is making my break with Palestine increasingly difficult. He enjoys my company, loves me after his fashion, but does not, for a moment, deny his allegiance to Lee. Which makes it all rather hopeless. Especially since marriage with Ellis, even if we were agreed to it, would be a definite step to unhappiness.

So I have left my job partly in anticipation of home-going, and partly since El Wad is finished and I find working as secretary for Beck at Mamillah Road dull and fatiguing. I have had a year of hard work through the summer without a vacation and now the wanderlust is on me. During the last three weeks, I have already taken three fascinating trips, one to Trans-Jordan, one to Kubeibi, a beautiful monastery in the hills west of Jerusalem, and one memorable hike to Marsaba, another monastery, in the desert southwest of Jerusalem. On the last trip, we were lost without water in the midday heat of the desert, but luckily we were directed by passing Bedouins to our destination which we reached

In the Transjordan (later called Jordan)

after an eight-hour hike. The same night we returned by the light of the stars alone, since it was the time of the new moon, through the wadis or gullies, following, in the darkness, the stony paths of dried streams. For miles before we came to Jerusalem, we saw her lights high upon the hill and, as the good-natured Bedouin played his wild flute-music for us, and we rested on a great flat rock, I saw how it had been that childlike peoples looked towards Jerusalem and saw in it the seat of God. It was a rich, beautiful experience, to be in the desert at night, and it was well worth the bitter fatigue we suffered.

Of Transjordan [later called Jordan], I must tell you, also—how we chartered an old ship and went around the Dead Sea, and then inland to magnificent canyons, to unleashed waterfalls bursting from the rocks, to fresh springs that made oases in the desert and to hot springs flinging themselves passionately (God save the word!) at the hearts of the great mountain boulders.

I have so much, so much to tell you, dearest girl-mine. I shall be coming soon, I think, probably the end of November or early December, since I plan for one or two weeks in Europe. I am so eager to see you.

My father, as you probably know, has sent me $175 but since some of it has gone and I feel it would be a great pity not to see Europe, I am going to ask Harry Neiman to lend me $50 if he can. I am sure you have been too hard up settling your own debts to have any spare money now. And I imagine I'll be able to repay Harry at not too late a date and not too high an interest.

Dear you and Joey, I shall see you both soon unless something <u>very</u> untoward happens, such as my changing my mind, etc.

Love!
Your Tzvia [Celia's Hebrew name]
Write American Express, Paris, unless I cable otherwise. I'll be here until about November 12. Celia

CITY ENGINEER'S DEPARTMENT
MUNICIPALITY OF JERUSALEM

Construction Manager
El Wad Sewer Reconstruction
Lawrence T. Beck A.M.I.C.E.

Jerusalem, 19 October, 1931

To Whom It May Concern:
Miss Celia Antopolsky acted as my private secretary during the whole
of the time that the above work was under construction.

I found her very concientious [*sic*] and hard working; in addition to
which I found her extremely discreet and examplary [*sic*] in her attention
to her duties and have no hesitation in recommending her for a similar
position where trust and concientiousness [*sic*] are essential.

(Signed) L. Beck
CONSTRUCTION MANAGER

Lillian to Celia (c/o American Express, Paris, France), November 15,
1931, picture postcard from Bear Mt. Inn N.Y.

There's a blazing fire, soft music—a
delightful end to a week-end in the open

Dear C.

Welcome to Paris and bon voyage! And soon, welcome home! The
news has travelled and you are anxiously awaited. Sorry I could not raise
the muzumah [cash] without asking your folks, but efforts of myself and
friends could not yield anything. Excitement reigns in your household

and your mother expects you any day. Cable her to meet the boat—she is looking forward to the pleasure. Your uncle Sholem states that he has a brother, Antopolsky, in Paris for 40 years. There's lots to tell you. And, incidentally, I hope it doesn't rain during your stay in Paris!

Love,

Lillian

Joey Marks to Celia (c/o American Express, Paris, France), November 15, 1931, picture postcard from Bear Mountain Inn

Dear Celia,

In this house and in front of the fireplace shown on the card Lily is sending by this mail, we have planned for our first reunion. So hurry, won't you and until then & always,

Yours affec.

JM

Celia to Lillian, December 5, 1931

Aboard Adria, Bound for Brindisi

My beloved chaverah Lillian

Have you excommunicated me altogether? My neck is on the block and you may chop it off or not as you will, but don't I beg you, cut me off from the charmed circle.

I have thought of you a million times. I have written to no one for the last few months because I have been in such a muddle of indecision. To go back to America and winter and no job, or to stay on indefinitely with the prospect of finding work here since I have already given up my job with Beck. Then the question of Ellis—Somehow, after the first few weeks, when Ellis's actions, I soon learned, were due to his bitter disappointment at my indifference, he seemed to turn about, adjust himself, and become the most charming companion anyone could want. The result was that we travelled everywhere together and found much joy as we had once planned, so that it was harder and harder for me to leave. He has been so wonderfully kind and considerate to me, even when I finally decided to leave, that I have only my old love and respect for him, but this time with no building for the future and a full realization of the situation. Ellis is but a shadow of himself. He has been under a terrific conflict during the last few months—on the one hand, his loyalty to Lee, on the other, his love for me. Whether he can let the situation rest as it is, I don't know. I know only that he did everything for me that a kind, fine man could do, and that my going means great pain to him. Already, he has sent me a telegram. So that's that. God knows what it will ever lead to.

Lillian, dearest, I have so much to tell you. I am constantly thinking that I am drawing nearer and nearer to you and I have deep joy at the thought.

Bremen, arr. Dec. 22 or 23. Until then, love to you and Joey.

Celia

Unmailed postcard (picture of Napoli) addressed to Lillian

Lillian, darling,

I'm coming closer. I find Italy fascinating and am loath to leave, but ever and anon, Kadimah! [Hebrew: Forward!]

Bremen, Dec. 22

Love you & J,
Celia

Chapter 26
So full a year as we have had
(Letter and telegram from Ellis Polonsky to Celia Antopolsky,
December 1 and 2, 1931)

Ellis to Celia, hand-delivered Tuesday, December 1, 1931, bearing
instruction: "To be opened Wed. at 3 p.m." [Note: Celia's ship, the Adria,
was scheduled to depart Haifa on Wednesday, December 2]

Comerado—

No one has been so gifted with so bright a comraderie as we have—no
one has had poured into their lives so full a year as we have had. Nothing
we can do can add or detract from its beauty and charm. Interwoven into
our companionship has been the intellectual and the emotional strain of
a relationship. At no time has the former caused us concern or difficulty.
The emotional strain has been the link that momentarily threatened the
entire fabric of our friendship. And that has been often predicted and
frankly expected.

Ruskin once said that "one never tires of intellectual attainments."
Everyone admits that emotional manifestations are constantly subject
to change and even absolute deterioration. Intellectually we have proven
ourselves as compatible as we have failed emotionally.

I, Marca, have failed to give what you emotionally desired. You have
suffered much and sacrificed a great deal. Our emotional philosophy has
failed of adjustment in these 2-1/2 years and seems to cause us to drift
further apart. You will never be happy with such an emotional arrange-

ment. Like the handwriting on the wall—It has been held in the balance and found wanting. We must now build up new emotional foundations to supplant the poorly grounded ones we have. We must come back emotionally free and intellectually stimulated.

Why have you interpreted my philosophy of emotional interest as being one of disinterest? How that would have simplified matters. How easily I could have ended things.

But care not, my comerado. Your ship is turned towards home where brothers and sisters await you and a new land is being built.

Lose yourself and our petty emotions with the mass emotions of the struggle of our people. Marca you are a daughter of an eternal people who are making their final struggle and you must help.

Rejoice in your homecoming—kiss the soil for me—say that I am coming. Stare into the hearts of your brothers and sisters and know why we say Am Yisroel Chai [the soul of the Jewish people lives].

Yod b'yod [hand in hand]
Ellis

PALESTINE POSTS, TELEGRAPHS & TELEPHONES
TELEGRAM

Handed in at Jerusalem
Time: 1851 on 2 [December 2]
Received at 2010
Haifa 2 DE 31

TO Antopolsky   Adria   Haifa

Broke promise am with you

Ellis

Chapter 27
This is how people go out of your life
(Letters from Ruth Light, a friend in Jerusalem, to Celia Antopolsky,
December 3, 1931 and January 31, 1932)

Letter to Celia from Ruth Light, December 3, 1931

Dear Celia—

It is the morning of the next day after you have left.

I am writing to Paris in the hope this will arrive before you reach there.

I am sure that by this time the rush of life, the new experiences, the new faces have washed away all remembrance of that last day you spent here, in Jerusalem.

Oh, it was a funny day, yesterday after you left. There stood Ellis, saying with a peculiar little smile,—"That is how people go out of your life,—on a train,—and that's all."

Mischa, Ellis and I went to the Lebanon for something to eat and we ordered

(over—paper is scarce)

cabbage soup and Ellis became sentimental and said "Gee, Celia used to love cabbage soup." Then we all laughed, of course, and that was that.

Then there came a squabble between Ellis and Mischa about the payment for the auto or something,—I don't know what. Anyway,—Mischa refused to accept any money for whatever it was and although Ellis tried to make him take it,—it was of no use.

So Celia, dear,—I tell you all these things to show you what a big space you have left in us,—in going.

I am afraid I am becoming, like Ellis, a little sentimental,—I had better be careful.

Look here, child,—do you know what I did yesterday in the excitement of things,—I took some good, needed, piastres and went and bought "The Road Back" [a novel by Erich Maria Remarque, published 1931]. I am sure I will have to walk to the Emek,—with all these extravagant break-outs of mine,—but I just had

(over—paper is still scarce)

to do something silly yesterday,—on that crazy day.

How are you enjoying Europe? I am sure if any one can, you are doing so this minute.

Paris must be a circus or bazaar or something. And Italy you must have loved. Its warmth (is it still warm at this season) and rich blood must be a delight to taste.

I am thinking of and preparing to leave Jerusalem these days,— perhaps in two or three weeks. Exactly where, don't know this minute.

Do write, Celia,—and soon,—too. Write me care of

J.N.F. [Jewish National Fund]
P.O. Box 283
Jerusalem
Palestine

They will forward mail to me.

Goodbye for the moment,—old thing,—enjoy yourself, be well,— don't buy too many presents or you may have to swim home.

Love,—and wishes of joy to you, –
Ruth Light

Ruth Light, typed letter to Celia, January 31, 1932

Dear Celia –

To say that I loved your letter is just the exact truth,—for it was a beautiful, colored cord strung cross the ocean bearing the peculiarly Celianess of the absent and longed-for Celia.

I do not think that a day passes in which we do not mention your name in one way or another. You left a dent in this distant land!

The "Americans" still continue to eat and to practice eating at Patt's. Here life is discussed; also gossip dispensed freely, glibly.

Water continues to be among the missing.

When your letter came I had to read most of it to the Shermans next whom I've been living these last two months,—Earl was wishing you had written a note to them, too. Have you seen their family yet?

Your mad almost-romance with the Latin was in keeping with what was bound to happen with you floating alone and unattached through strange, new lands. I wonder about the poor little lover—what kind of complex did you leave him with? you the social worker! For we know of your great good fortune in finding work on your arrival. How you did it with conditions being what they are—is a mystery to us and still not so entirely insoluble too. All the same you are a lucky kid!

Ellis has finally been forced into almost working, he teaches English and when his pupils, who seem to like his lessons, try to form new classes for him he becomes most annoyed and manages to escape in some manner. He is remarkable in his ingenious methods for escaping.

By this time you must be entirely in tune with your new life in America again and awake to new experiences. Which is good. The need for change is a peculiar part of man and while it is often disagreeable to change it is often best. That sounds something like moralizing, doesn't it? Don't know how it happened, I swear.

Write as soon as you can, Celia dear, I will like so much hearing from you. Tell me how you are finding your new work—and all else.

The gang always asks news of you and wants to know when letters come. So for many reasons write. And mostly because I want to hear from you.

With love.

Ruth

Postcard from Damascus, postmarked April 6, 1932
Addressed to Celia Antopolsky at 248 Liberty Ave., Brooklyn, N.Y.,
U.S.A.

I have turned East before I turn West.
Syria has the green that our land cries for.

Ellis

Chapter 28
The American girl from Jerusalem

Carte Postale *addressed to Miss Celja Antopolsky c/o American Express,*
Paris:

Dear Celja!
    We are very glad to hear that you are coming to Paris. We are still
more glad to see you. So please come tomorrow the 15 Decembre at half
past eight in the evening to our house. We will be waiting for you.

Yours friendly
Nina Zucker

—⁊⁊—

From Brindisi, Italy, Celia took a train to Paris, and spent two nights
with her friends there, two French girls she had met in Palestine. Both of
the French girls had to go to work during the day, and were so lucky to
have jobs that they couldn't claim any privilege such as taking the day off.
But that was all right with Celia because the day was the only time she
could sleep.
    While in Jerusalem, the girls had seemed on the fringe of Celia's
social group—with Celia at the center, the group had been almost a
reprise of the group that had surrounded her in college and, even more
so, later when she and Lillian had lived in the Apartment. Although—

and this was the crucial difference, she thought—her group in Jerusalem had not been composed of creative people, and therefore, although she was at the center of it, it was not really *her* group. The first night, she took a taxi from the railroad station to the girls' apartment—and how nice, how civilized, to be able to hire an actual taxicab as in New York, instead of having to scramble to hire one of the odd assortment of vehicles for hire in Palestine, driven by who knows who and who knew in what condition—not that Celia could afford many taxis on her limited budget, but she allowed herself this one. The girls, big smiles on their faces, showing their teeth—odd that she had never noticed their teeth, which were large and yellow behind bright red lipstick—greeted her with a barrage of French before remembering that she was not quite one of them and needed to be addressed in English, still a foreign tongue to them although they both spoke it quite well, but the point was that she was a bit exotic to them even after all the time they had spent together in Jerusalem. Celia was tired after her long train ride, but she was to have no rest yet, because the girls had other company. Into the little apartment were crowded ten or twelve of their Paris friends, eager to meet the American girl from Jerusalem. Some appeared not even to be Jewish; all seemed slim and sophisticated, city folk, with their cigarettes and their glasses of wine. The two girls also, now that she looked closely at them, had already morphed into their Parisian personas, and moved about with subtle slinks instead of the healthy strides of youths in Palestine.

But after a few minutes of uncertainty, someone put a glass of wine in her hand, and everyone started speaking in English out of consideration for her, and asking questions about America and about her adventures in Palestine, where she had stayed much longer than her hostesses; and then she understood who she was and was happy to have a role in this gathering. She was the exotic foreigner, and therefore everything she said was fascinating; recognizing this, she relaxed and told them stories of Palestine and of hitchhiking across the United States the year before, and they were eager to listen, and the party went on until late at night. Finally, Celia went to bed in her clothes on the sofa before the last guest had left, as she couldn't keep her eyes open another minute, and drifted into sleep lulled by the soft voices of the French-speakers.

In the late afternoon of the following day (it was only an hour earlier in Palestine), Celia finally bestirred herself to arise, shower, and wander into the tiny kitchen where the girls had left her a croissant and some jam. She heated leftover coffee on the stove and drank it sitting at the small table in the living room that served also as a desk for the girls, stacks of newspapers and mail and magazines covering one side of it. In a bookcase were a handful of contemporary books in French, English, and Hebrew.

She had only a couple of hours before the girls came home, looking forward to entertaining her. Only two free hours in Paris. She could rush to the Louvre, if she could figure out how to get there, and spend an hour looking at great art. Or she could walk out, find a coffee shop, sit outside and try to read a French newspaper. In the end, that was what she did, and fantasized that she lived there all the time, that somehow she had absorbed the Parisian sense of style, casual and cheap but knowing, wise with centuries of civilization. Maybe in Paris she could write, anonymous at her table outside the coffee shop, except she was getting a bit chilly; it was December after all, and she might just go inside, and then she noticed that most of the people in that particular coffee shop were solitary, drinking their coffees and reading their newspapers or staring into space, and not writing at all, and she shivered and went back to the apartment, arriving shortly before the girls who were eager to take her out to dinner with a half dozen of their friends, and then it was a repeat of the first night, toasts to America and France and Palestine, *boeuf bourguignon* and *beignets*, red wine, and a tipsy return to the apartment and earnest conversation about world peace and the writing life and a life of adventure: which was better? Could a woman do either; should a woman do either? And, in the end, not much sleep for Celia, who had to get up early the next morning, coffee and croissants and tearful *au revoirs*, though they all knew, they must have known, that they would never see each other again.

Chapter 29
Fourteen days on that boat

The third-class accommodations on the *Bremen* were not so bad. True, they lacked privacy, but it was not for so very long, and that way she was protected from dwelling too much on the absence of Ellis and Lillian.

The personas, she remembered with nostalgia, that she and Ellis had sent across the ocean to each other, twining together over the waves— she had to mourn them too, as if they had been real people. She had been Ellis's Queen, his princess, his lover, and they would go hand in hand like lost children throughout Europe. And for her part, she had been the bright butterfly who flitted eternally from one adventure to the next. Yes, there had been something childlike about both of them. Only children lived entirely in the present.

She looked through a porthole, out across the wintry ocean. There was no time for nostalgia. She had 14 days on that boat, and during those two weeks she had to decide who she was, who she was going to be. She couldn't bear to think what it would be like to emerge from her voyage with no sense of how she wanted to present herself to her family, to her friends, whoever yet remained to her. Perhaps even Lillian was lost to her, because Joey would probably be loyal to his friend Ellis, and Celia would be eased out of the group, perhaps without anyone having planned or intended it, but because it would be too awkward to have Ellis and Celia together.

The sudden thought of Harry Neiman made her laugh. Good old Harry, earnest and innocent. He had a picture of her in his mind, the very picture she had tried to convey, the very same image of herself that she had believed would enable her to charm any man she liked. Maybe it would only work to attract an innocent like Harry. It had never—she decided now—never worked with Ellis. He had seen through her from the beginning, and besides, he'd been too busy creating an image of himself for her eyes.

She must decide what she was like and do it quickly. Fourteen days.

The childlike appreciation of what was whimsical and imaginative: She wanted to keep that; she hoped she would never become so adult as to lose that.

The creative spirit. She was a creator, a visualizer. During her stay in Palestine she had been preoccupied with Ellis and other men. That had been a mistake. She had failed to keep up her writing, which was her essence, and she had not even kept a journal to help remember the experiences that could form the core of future writings. She would resume her creative work and recapture her sense of herself as an observer who saw everything with unique vision, who could convey her understanding to others in ways that could stir them, even break their hearts. She would move through the world alone, never losing her stance as seer and voice.

She would regain the self-assurance she had felt in college and in the Apartment. She would remember who she was and that she did not depend on anyone else to make her who she was.

She would have to find some kind of job. Either that or stay home taking care of Mama, which would please Betty, but, oh dear, she would waste away cooped up in that house. She must face the truth: She was not the kind of person who lived to take care of others.

She had a very strong feeling that she hadn't gotten it yet, whatever it was that she had the capacity, the potential, the talent, the inclination to get from life. She was uniquely talented, people always said so; and life did have something in store for her—not automatically, not assuredly, but potentially in store, like a gift waiting in a hidden place. So she had to remember about it, and keep looking for it, and working for it, because otherwise she would never find it and her life would be a failure, an opportunity missed. She could not abandon her search in order to care for someone else's needs.

The alternative was the realm of the nurse, the nun, the woman behind a successful man, the spinster caring for an aged mother, the mother tending day and night to a demanding child. She wouldn't get herself trapped like that.

The bed nearest hers in the third-class sleeping quarters was occupied by an English lady going to visit her son in America. She had settled in Palestine, but he had made a different choice and now lived in California where he was hoping to get into the young movie industry.

"Come out on deck, why don't you?" the lady said. "You'll feel better. Are you sad about something, dear?"

"No," said Celia to the English lady. "I just wanted to be by myself to think for a while. I'm all right now."

"Did you get it all figured out, then?"

"Yes. I did."

Yes, she had figured it out. She had moved through a time of grief and despair but at last had remembered who she was. When she met others, she wanted them to see immediately, or very soon, what she was like: a charming woman, still young, and educated, and talented beyond any doubt, and with some experience of the world.

Soon she would have to start lying about her age. She was almost twenty-six and it was a little odd: People would wonder why she had neither married nor embarked on a career. Why hadn't she thought of that before, all those months after Lillian had left, when Celia stayed behind waiting for Ellis like a fool; why had she not known that the time remaining to her was something less than infinite? But never mind: She was still young and must appear so, because everyone and especially men wanted to help a charming woman, as long as she was young and bright-eyed.

Standing at the rail on the last day, she looked out at the gray December sea, her mood almost the opposite of what it had been when she and Lillian had traveled in the other direction. It was hard to recapture the hopeful resolves of even a few days before. She was separated—possibly forever—from Lillian, her best friend and traveling companion, and from Ellis, who might turn out to have been the love of her life. She was heading toward a cold New York winter, with no job and no prospects, only a single scrap of paper with the phone number of a shipboard acquaintance's cousin who could maybe get her a job as a social worker. Pater, who had published her poems the year before, seemed to have lost all his money or at any rate was unable or unwilling to pay for the works he had already published. The old group of friends was scattered, and even those still in New York were working at whatever jobs they could find and wouldn't be available anymore for carefree socializing. She envisioned long days doing social work in the slums of Brooklyn, evenings caring for her sick mother and writing letters.

There was a shout behind her: The skyline of New York City was just barely visible through a dense fog. The passengers, bundled into warm coats, crowded the rail as the ship neared the dock. Celia scanned the crowd of relatives and friends. There she saw her mother and her sister Minna, and was Minna pregnant? And there was Lillian. And Harry Neiman, of all people, holding what looked like a small bouquet of flowers. Red roses. Where could Harry have found roses in the middle of winter? They must have cost a fortune—how could he have afforded it? She smiled. *Such a foolish, romantic boy*, she would say to Lillian; *whatever shall I do with him?*

The boat had docked and the passengers were spilling out. She fixed her face into an expression of delighted welcome, and joined the others descending into the city.

Chapter 30
Afterword

After taking a break for another year, Ellis picked up his life where he
had left it. He returned to the United States, remained married to
Lee, built a career out of his work for Jewish organizations, and died of a
heart attack in 1955 at the age of fifty-one. He and Lee had one child.

Lillian, also, found her previous life waiting for her. She married Joey,
who became a vice-president of Doubleday Publishing Company. She did
social work, taught in the public schools, and wrote a manual for teaching
touch-typing. She and Joey returned to Palestine (later Israel) many times to
visit and teach. They had three children. Lillian died in 2015 at the age of 107.

Mama Antopolsky continued to suffer from asthma but lived on until
1946, surviving her husband by several years and dying at age seventy.

Betty used the cooking skills her mother had taught her to open and
operate a delicatessen in Brooklyn which supported her, her husband, and
their daughter.

Minna's marriage to Al ended in divorce. Neither of them remarried.
They had one child.

Irving (Ike) never practiced law. He married, owned an office furniture
store, and had three children.

—∞—

Celia soon found a job doing social work with the Jewish Family
Welfare Society, the same agency that employed Lillian, although not

in the same office. She knew she was lucky to have a job, but felt there was no real point to it. What did social work have to do with charming roomsful of people? With writing poetry that astounded readers with its lyrical perfection?

The suitors were gone, all but Harry Neiman, whose affection was so flattering that she couldn't bear to let him go. But she couldn't quite bring herself to accept him either, and postponed the decision.

She had no rational reason to turn him down. He was good-looking and likable. He was a lawyer, better equipped than most to make a good living. He didn't make her heart beat faster as Ellis had, but there would never be another Ellis.

The trouble was that Harry's idealized view of her as a poetic free spirit was so at odds with the wry and insecure person she knew herself to be. She had only herself to blame. This was the image she had fostered, and which, even now, she perpetuated.

He wrote:

> We cannot go on like this. I demand something definite, concrete, sure. I have had enough of half promises, half hearted guarded reciprocation . . . maybes, . . . perhaps, . . . somedays, . . . oh gee, I don't know, . . . wait 'til spring, . . . wait 'til after I get back from Palestine,. . . . I almost love you,. . . .I think I love you ,. . . . sometimes I think I love you etc. etc., until I am emotionally dizzy and unable to carry on effectually at the office or elsewhere.

They were married at last, Celia and Harry, on September 6, 1933, in the apartment of Lillian and Joey, who served as witnesses. The wedding was so informal, and felt so spontaneous, that she could almost delude herself into thinking she still had her freedom. She could get a Mexican divorce, Harry said, in twenty-four hours. They were so free-floating that they moved to a different apartment every year on May 1, which, by custom, was Moving Day in New York.

Moving Day was gloriously chaotic; it seemed that everyone in the city was moving out of one apartment into another that had just been vacated by someone else, in a grand game of musical chairs. To Harry, each move represented a fresh start. Celia liked the lack of permanence, the bohemian atmosphere. She bought a red blown-glass vase and later, three tiny oriental rugs to carry with them.

When she became pregnant, she persuaded the Antopolskys' family doctor, who had known her all her life, to perform an illegal abortion. It didn't occur to her that she might avoid childbearing altogether, but she intended to postpone it as long as possible. "When we want a child, we'll have one," she wrote to Harry. She continued to use her maiden name.

She took voice lessons. Maybe she could be an opera singer.

—∿—

Harry needed to be constantly reassured that she loved him, as if words could change the reality!

But maybe they could, she thought. Maybe as she wrote words of love she would come to feel the truth of them.

Celia to Harry, April, 1934

> [I think of] the fine clean face of my man, his dear brown eyes, his fragrant hair, and his good, young body. Were you here, darling mine, you would still be the handsomest man at the Conference, and, I think, the most charming! . . . I would be the sea, dear, so that each time I make a forward movement, I could take back some part of you. Harinka, my beloved . . . My love for you is grown deep, rooted in the depths of me—just try and pull loose!

He resolved to write to her every time they were separated overnight, and did so, letters filled with protestations of love, which she mirrored in her less frequent letters to him.

Celia to Harry, July 5, 1938

Beloved man of mine—

. . . So all your dear, ardent, earnest, loyal, rock-of-Gibraltar, clever-as-hell letters are not the breath of life to me? No, except that they make me warm all over, and that I think of you again and again both day and night, and that I do love you, love you, love you—more than you will ever believe or, perhaps, understand.

—⁓—

She was losing touch with her old friends, all busy with work or school or both. The past relationship between Celia and Ellis complicated efforts to socialize with Lillian and Joey, because Ellis and Joey remained good friends.

They were invited to parties given by members of Celia's old crowd. She greeted the men by kissing them. Harry objected. His wife shouldn't be kissing another man on the mouth. She refused to stop. The kissing meant nothing; it was customary among those people. In which case, Harry didn't approve of those people. Because the dispute flared after every party and could not be resolved, they stopped going to the parties.

Her friendships with people she had met in her travels across the country and in Palestine and Europe were also fading. It took time and energy to write a good letter. People wrote to her, hopeful, lively letters, asking her to send them another letter like the delightful one she had previously written to them. The standard set by the previous letter would have to be met or exceeded. What was the point, when she had already proved herself?

Harry wrote to a friend, apologizing on her behalf:

You must know how writers are—you know, they literally have to give birth to even the simplest of communications, weigh each word, erase it, move it over, back, erase again,

get temperamental, then put the letter off another month
. . . Celia's not like that, not exactly, but you know what I
mean—writing as such means so much and is so hard that
one just keeps putting it off.

Whereas, he wrote, because he was not a writer, he was free to pick up a pen and scrawl any old thing.

He tried to be her conscience with respect to letter-writing. When Celia was away at a summer-camp job, he urged her to write to her mother and to Lillian and to another couple who were old friends.

Ah, dear child, I seek only to keep you in the good graces of
those who will be reproachful later . . . Nor do I care about
the others, <u>as you know</u>. But I do care about you, your happi-
ness, and that's why I feel you should write one letter to each
and maybe several to mother during the summer.

In the end, it was too hard. She stopped writing letters almost entirely, except for letters to Harry. Friends she had made in the past dropped out of her life.

—⚹—

Harry struggled to make money in his law practice. She told him he undercharged his clients. He insisted he charged as much as they could afford to pay. She said he cared more for the needs of others—his clients, his father's creditors (he continued to try to pay off his father's debts)—than for the needs of himself and his wife.

He was determined to make good on his promise to support her so that she would be free to write.

Now it has boiled down to a question of courage. I must work,
suffer, persevere and work, work, work if I hope to support
you and give you your chance. You must have that chance
and it will be on my conscience if I don't give it to you.

He took to calling her "little girl," "childy," and "kiddie" in his letters, until finally she told him how much she hated it.

By 1937, she had been working for five years at the social work job that she had thought of as only temporary. Her supervisor at the Jewish Family Welfare Society urged her to pursue a graduate degree in social work, so that she could do counseling. The agency would pay. She applied to the New York School of Social Work. Filling out the application triggered self-doubt. A few years before, she had failed the exam that would have qualified her to be a public school teacher. Maybe this career also would be closed to her.

After being admitted, she wrote:
> *I realize now that the worry about the school's decision has been in me all the time, tight underneath, put away from consciousness. I feel more at ease now; free, perhaps, from the spectre fear-of-failure that haunts us all, but particularly me.*

She continued to take courses toward the master's degree, completing most of the requirements, until World War II and the birth of her daughter, in April 1942, changed everything.

———

She had consented to bear a child at the age of thirty-six, after almost a decade of postponement during her marriage. Her father, Aaron Antopolsky, was in poor health and wanted her to give him a grandchild before he died. Besides, each of her sisters had already achieved motherhood—one child apiece—and her childless condition, she sensed, diminished her status in the family.

The schedule didn't quite work out as planned, because Aaron died before the baby was born. But the timing was excellent in another way. Being married and a father at just that time put Harry into a category (it was soon eliminated) that exempted him from the draft during the war, a stroke of good fortune that may well have saved his life.

She stopped working, to care for the baby. She had always fulfilled assignments with excellence, and now that she had a child, she intended to do an excellent job of raising it.

Indeed, she did intuitively know what later science confirmed, that talking to a baby helps develop language skills. She held long "conversations" with the baby that mystified Harry, and claimed to believe that the baby really understood her.

Soon after their daughter was born, Harry and Celia made what, in retrospect, was a spectacularly unfortunate decision. It was July, and a terrific heat wave struck New York City. They felt it was essential—for the baby's sake if not for their own—that they get out of the city for the summer.

An acquaintance told them of a room for rent in Seagate, at the western tip of Coney Island. Celia wrote, in an unfinished letter to a friend:

> *Harry rushes to Seagate. He finds not one, but two rooms with a terrace. What matter if the terrace is only a second-story porch and that you have to step through a window to get to it? What if the kitchen has a leaky ice-box and gaping screens? It's only for the summer, and for that it is luxury. Besides, the seashore is there, and the sun, and if the season is half-over, the landlady does not notice this and charges rent as though it were the beginning of June. The illusion is perfect.*

They gave up their current apartment in Brooklyn Heights, put most of their furniture in storage, and set up housekeeping in the two-room apartment in Seagate. The time there didn't go well. The heat wave broke and the rest of the summer was rainy and cold; there seemed no escape from the chill damp. Harry's commute to the city was two hours each way. The apartment was uncomfortable and the landlady was an unpleasant person who made a business of hosting women's poker parties in her home—an activity that was not only unladylike but low-class (and Celia ought to know; hadn't her father hosted a poker party for the Antopolskys' immigrant relatives every Sunday?). But it was only at the end of the summer, when they tried to return to New York, that the full disastrousness of the move revealed itself.

There were no apartments to be had. They had been accustomed to the lively chaos of Moving Day and the ready availability of apartments all year round. But the war had caused shortages of construction materials and labor. To ration the existing apartments, rent controls were imposed. Landlords were prohibited from raising rent except in specified circumstances (such as renting the apartment to a new tenant). That created an incentive for tenants to stay in their current apartments rather than accept a price hike to move to another. The tradition of Moving Day, which had dated to colonial times, was gone, never to be revived.

They ended up in an apartment at 190th Street and Broadway in Washington Heights, near the George Washington Bridge at the northern tip of Manhattan, which they were able to snag only because the former occupants, Harry's sister and her family, were moving out of town.

Fortunately, Celia didn't know at the time that the move to Washington Heights was to rank as one of the landmark events in her life. Especially because it was conflated with the birth of her daughter, it was the kind of occurrence that puts everything that happens into one of the two categories "before" and "after."

Physically, the apartment was adequate. It had a living room, kitchen, bathroom, dining area and two bedrooms. It was on the highest floor, the sixth, and the building was on a hill so that the large windows in Harry and Celia's bedroom had a beautiful view, looking across the expanse of Broadway to a park on the other side. It was a corner room so the windows faced in two directions and could be opened to let in a hint of a breeze on even the hottest day.

But Celia hated the place from the beginning. Unlike the famous Apartment, Celia and Lillian's "salon" on downtown Madison Street, the Washington Heights apartment was distant by the full length of Manhattan from friends, work, and cultural institutions. Worse, the neighborhood in which they were marooned was populated by first-generation German Jews, an insular group that clung to their old customs and looked with scorn on Jews like Celia whose families had come from Eastern Europe. She could expect no friendship among those people. She tried to look on the bright side. It was in the city at least, and surely something better would come along.

Except that it didn't. The apartment in Washington Heights would remain Harry and Celia's home for the next thirty-four years. The reason was economic: They could never afford to move. Because of rent control, that apartment remained always their cheapest option.

—⚌—

Harry wasn't making enough in his law practice to support his wife and child. By the early 1940s, he recognized that his business was unlikely to improve, and regretfully stopped practicing law. He followed the suggestion of a relative who was familiar with the garment industry and became a fur jobber, buying fur coats from manufacturers in New York and selling to retailers in several New England cities.

Marketing the coats was time-consuming. He transported them in person, packed in special large boxes, by train to Philadelphia and other cities. Then he called on retailers in the fur district of each city, carrying the boxes with him. At night he wrote to Celia from his hotel room, reporting on the day—how many retailers he'd visited, whether he'd made any sales. Profit on a coat was small, maybe $15. Celia tried to help keep his spirits up. Maybe he could succeed in this odd niche.

He no longer had a suite, or even a room, in an office building. A fur manufacturer in New York allowed Harry, as a favor, to use his address. Adjacent to the manufacturer's showroom, in a large open area under fluorescent lights, eight skilled men, all Greek immigrants, cut up mink skins and sewed them into coats, capes, and scarves; that was the factory.

The train travel proved strenuous and impractical. Determined to make a success of the venture, Harry learned to drive and actually bought a car (a novelty for city folk). After some experimenting, his schedule became fairly well fixed. He would leave the apartment every Wednesday morning and return on Saturday evening, exhausted. He took Sunday off, visited manufacturers on Monday and Tuesday, and left again on Wednesday.

His schedule didn't allow for a very active social life for him and Celia. That was unfortunate, but to some extent it was a relief for Celia. Despite the front she presented, socializing had never come easily to her. She had to get in the mood for every encounter, because she felt it was incumbent on her to be the life of every gathering. She decided she was basically a "loner," happy to be at home working on her writing.

She no longer wrote poetry. The money was in short stories. Mass circulation magazines like *Collier's* and *Harper's Bazaar* would pay well enough that she could afford to spend full time at her writing. That is, if only they would buy her stories.

She bought a desk from her brother Irving's office furniture store, positioned it in the living room—the only available place in the apartment— and typed and retyped page after page on her manual typewriter. Alternative drafts of stories were scattered about the living room in little piles.

—⁂—

As Celia had feared, after several years it was apparent that the fur business would be no more lucrative for Harry than the practice of law had been. But he kept trying, knowing no other option than to keep doing what he had been doing, only harder.

She hired a sitter to watch the child every day while she finished the thesis for her master's in social work. She earned the degree but didn't want to work full time while her daughter was still young, so she got a job as a substitute teacher in the New York public schools. She was a "permanent sub," meaning that she worked every day with the same class, just like a regular teacher. It was a high-school course in Pitman stenography, which she had never learned. She stayed a chapter ahead of the class. The trick, as always, was never to admit that she didn't know.

During the summer breaks, she worked at children's camps as a Dramatics counselor (she wrote original plays for the children to perform) or an Arts and Crafts counselor (knowing nothing of traditional crafts, she had the children make crepe-paper flowers and paint murals). In exchange for reduced pay, she arranged for her daughter to attend the camp as a regular camper.

—⁓—

Lacking the specific certification required, but possessed of her master's in social work and a creative imagination, Celia managed eventually to become a guidance counselor at the junior high school level. She held that position until she retired, serving in two different schools. During her stint at a school in a poor neighborhood, she had unusual success in getting her students admitted to the most demanding high schools in the city (the Bronx High School of Science and the High School of Music and Art). She even wrote an article about young teenagers that was published in *Parents Magazine*.

—⁓—

Without fully acknowledging it, she had come to understand that she would not be doing creative writing. Not poetry, her first love, or even fiction. True, she had a career, but she had failed to fulfill her promise. It was overwhelming to think of all she might have written and now would never write—letters, poems, stories, novels, a universe of brilliance within her that would never be released.

Her attention shifted to managing the impression she made on others. She took to reciting her youthful exploits ("I hitchhiked across the country!"), sometimes exaggerating for emphasis ("I lived for two years in Palestine!").

How she dressed, how she presented herself to the world was important. Even to walk across the street to the Safeway supermarket, she had to dress as if she were going to teach a class. What if she ran into one of her students?

Her appearance had to send several, possibly inconsistent, messages. She couldn't wear anything so unconventional that it would shock the ordinary people. But for those with eyes to see, she wore distinctive accessories—a scarf or pin of odd design, earrings that were handmade or seemed to be—subtle signals of her artistic taste. And of course she must not try to look as if she thought she were pretty or glamorous, or she would become pitiable, a laughingstock. She shopped in downscale department stores and prided herself on being able to spot items of clothing or costume jewelry that, though inexpensive, were *unusual*—her highest accolade.

It took time to assemble the right outfit. Even for a Sunday drive in the country she might take two hours or more to apply careful makeup and select what to wear, trying on several outfits, uncertain which was best. They would be eating lunch in some roadside restaurant, a Howard Johnson's perhaps. Who knew whom they might run into?

Harry and their daughter laughed at her. "I am a rose between two thorns," she said. Making a joke, hiding the hurt. And she refused to hurry.

—⚬—

One of Harry's business friends praised Celia: "She has such good humor. A woman like that is a help to a man. I don't think she's ever sad."

Harry repeated the praise in a letter to Celia, adding: "Sweet dear one, everyone loves you, except women of course."

It was true. Men, by and large, liked Celia. Women, by and large, didn't.

She had little in common with most of them. All they cared about were recipes and fashion and homemaking tips, things she knew nothing about. Things she was proud of knowing nothing about; why busy herself with such trivia?

Sometimes she tried to talk to them on their level, feigning interest: asking, for instance, for a recipe she had no intention of preparing.

It would have been better, she sometimes thought, had she been born a man.

She bought a 9x12 oriental rug for the living room. When the landlord reluctantly agreed to have the apartment painted, she insisted the painters mix the colors to her satisfaction. But no matter what she did, the apartment was never nice enough to be seen by anyone but the family. It was the location, she thought, that couldn't be overcome. Or it was lack of money. Or it was just that she didn't know, ahead of time, what a given person's reaction would be. To ask someone to travel all the way to Washington Heights and not be able to present them with something special was embarrassing. And besides, she didn't know what to serve.

But Harry's schedule made entertaining impossible anyway.

—∞—

She had nothing to show for all those years of effort.

How had it happened? For one thing, the Depression had dried up opportunities and made living simply a matter of survival for many. Then came World War II, which had brought about the rent control law that had never been repealed, imprisoning them for practical purposes in an apartment she had hated from the beginning, an apartment that was so far north that people thought she lived in the Bronx and not Manhattan.

And there was the child. Her daughter, whose presence had hamstrung her for so many years, and into whose upbringing she had poured so much conscientious effort, had grown up, married, moved far away. In her weekly phone calls the daughter was stilted and distant, revealing as little of herself as possible. Celia bragged to acquaintances about her daughter's accomplishments, concealing the pain of rejection.

But the main target, the butt of her fury, was her husband, in her eyes a well-meaning softy who had no imagination, no vision. She had married the wrong man; it had been wrong from the beginning; she ought to have known better. She started to write an article, "Don't marry a man who. . . ."

A mama's boy, with four adoring sisters. Trying to make everybody love him instead of taking care of his family. A failure at the law, a failure in the fur business. Why didn't he charge more—so what if he lost a customer? He would make more from the others. He was afraid to take a chance. Look how well Joey Marks had done, and he had started with nothing.

She told him. Every night she told him.

—⁂—

It was hard to believe he was still faithful to her. As good-looking as he still was, as plain as she had always been. All those nights away from home. All those women in Philadelphia, Hartford, Boston who found him so charming. One of the furriers had asked Harry to work for him in the store because the retail customers liked him so much. But Harry, for his part, said he hated to deal with their indecision, their need for flattery.

A husband and wife in Hartford, Mr. and Mrs. Weiner, befriended Harry and invited him to spend the night when he was in town, which he did every week for years. He liked the Weiners. And it saved the cost of a restaurant meal and a night at a hotel.

All those home-cooked meals, and a well-ordered household that could easily accommodate a stranger's visit: Mrs. Weiner must have seemed, to Harry, like the ideal wife he'd never had. He was probably in love with Mrs. Weiner. And she with him, because Celia knew how he turned on the charm with women. He had always been that way; he almost couldn't help it. That sincere, boyish look. That self-deprecating smile. People always liked Harry. They liked his sincerity and his interest in what they had to say. If they only knew.

Her worry spilled over into accusations: joking, at first, offhand re-marks that could be disavowed as not serious. But the more she repeated them the more real they became. Maybe it wasn't Mrs. Weiner. Maybe it was some receptionist, some customer. There were so many women he came into contact with.

Even at home, it might be some woman he met in the elevator, some-one they passed on the street. She saw his eyes, how they took in a woman, registered her appearance.

Her accusations never failed to trigger passionate denials, avowals that he loved her and only her, and always had. It was good to hear his denials, but could she quite believe them? Wasn't he protesting too much? She of all people knew how easy it was to feign love.

—∿—

In a desperate act of self-assertion, at the age of 70, she packed up and moved away from the apartment in Washington Heights. She was retired and independent with a pension and Social Security as well as the savings she had squirreled away from her salary over the years, keeping the accounts in her name alone; there would have been no sense in leaving them available for Harry's creditors. She had prudently insisted that Harry pay their living expenses while she saved her money, because wasn't it his job to support her?

Her sister Betty's daughter, Joanie, lived in an apartment in Chevy Chase, Maryland, in a beautiful building with a carpeted lobby and a doorman. Celia had always wanted to live in a building like that. Joanie helped her find an apartment in the building to rent.

Harry refused to move. He didn't want to leave his sisters in New York, and he still kept his business going as well as he could, although the doctor said he should take it easy. He had a heart condition, and macular degeneration.

She left the old furniture but took the oriental rugs. She packed her clothing, her books, her papers—all the letters, all the drafts, and boxes of raw material for stories and books that she might write sometime—about Palestine, about teaching, about being a guidance counselor. Harry drove her from New York to Chevy Chase, trying all the time to persuade her to change her mind.

In Chevy Chase, Joanie helped her select and buy all new furniture—living room, bedroom, study, dining room. On her first night in the new apartment, Celia tore a photo of Harry in half and put the pieces in an envelope. She wrote a note: "This day marks the end of my first marriage," and put it into the envelope with the photo.

For the first time in her life, she was living in a place she could be proud of. But still, she invited no one to visit. There was no one to invite. She didn't know anyone in town but Joanie, and after a few weeks she and Joanie had a big argument, and she remembered that she had never been close to Joanie anyway.

She was lonely. Harry, still in New York, wrote that he too was lonely. She wrote that she was sure she could take care of him.

A year and a half after Celia's big move, Harry came for a visit on Thanksgiving weekend and didn't go back. He phoned his sister and asked her to break up the old apartment in Washington Heights.

They were in a new place, but little else had changed. There were the same health problems, the same lack of friends, the same history of failure and disappointment.

Soon, Celia's anger bubbled over again. Harry begged her to be kind, to "be a friend." Every night, when she put in his eye drops, she wrenched his head back so far that it hurt.

—⁓—

Her off-the-wall accusations and nightly rants of recrimination should have been warning signals, but Harry took them at face value, as he had always taken the things she said, and tried to counter them by reasonable argument and appeals to human kindness. She was so clever, so skilled at deflecting awkward questions, so capable of orienting herself quickly to whatever situation she found herself in, even when she didn't quite know how she'd gotten there, that several years passed before Harry and I understood that she was suffering from serious memory loss, both short- and long-term. The cause was multi-infarct dementia, or many small strokes, because of untreated high blood pressure.

Harry had been diagnosed with Alzheimer's disease by then. After a medical crisis forced me to put him into a nursing home near where I lived, it became clear that Celia, too, needed a more structured environment. She lived in a retirement home for several months but her old difficulty with deciding what to wear, aggravated by short-term memory loss, meant that she was unable to dress herself in order to come downstairs for meals. Eventually, I moved Celia into the same nursing home Harry was in, and arranged for them to be together in the same room.

At first, both were delighted to be together again. Perhaps Celia would have reverted to her old scolding pattern after a while, but they weren't together long enough for that to happen.

His balance was poor and it was dangerous for him to try to walk unattended, but her dementia was such that she couldn't understand his limitations and thought he should be allowed to move about freely. The result was a fall and a broken hip. They had been roommates for less than twenty-four hours.

When he came back from the hospital, Harry was put in a separate room. Both Harry and Celia had vision and hearing problems on top of dementia. Although the staff and I tried to bring them together during the day, it grew ever harder for them to communicate or even be aware of each other's presence.

Harry died two years later, but Celia was in vigorous physical health and lived a total of ten years in the nursing home. As the years passed, memory loss smoothed away the prickly parts of her personality. She became nicer, more friendly and accepting. She stopped making derogatory comments about staff and fellow residents, and smiled at the aides as they tended to her.

"She's my helper," she would say of an aide. "My good friend. I don't know what I'd do without her."

Maybe she was being manipulative, trying to stay on the good side of the nursing home staff. But I like to think she simply forgot to assume that others were judging her harshly. I like to think she achieved that degree of peace.

She still claimed, vaguely, to remember Harry.

"He was a sweet guy," she said.

ACKNOWLEDGEMENTS

Thanks to the members of my writing group for suffering through various versions: Kendra Hayden, Emily Spreng Lowery, Patti McCarty, and Jeannine Vesser. Thanks to Catherine Rankovic for her skillful editing and for clarifying the focus of this manuscript. Thanks to Bob Saigh, whose nagging got me started on the first draft.

Thanks to Rabbi Yosef Landa for translating some Yiddish passages. Posthumous thanks to Lillian Shapiro Marks (1907–2015) for many long conversations that helped me understand the events to which this book bears witness.

And thanks to my mother for saving every letter she ever received, on the chance that someone, sometime, would make use of them.

A NOTE ABOUT SOURCES

The letters are genuine. I have made trivial corrections in grammar, spelling, and punctuation, and deleted some passages that were neither particularly interesting nor relevant to the story line. Items that are given attribution (poems, transcribed documents, excerpts from articles or books) are genuine. However, some names have been changed.

All other conversations, events, and reflections were written by me.

I am not a historian. Any error of fact or inference regarding historical events is inadvertent and I apologize for it.

The family stories in Chapter 12 are essentially as told to me by my parents and other relatives and by Celia's friend Lillian.

The events in the final chapter ("Afterword") were pieced together by me from my own recollections, conversations with Lillian and others, letters from my parents to each other in years following the period covered by this book, and other documents such as applications, transcripts, and letters from other people.

Throughout, I have tried to be true to the reality of Celia's life as I have come to understand it in the course of writing this book.

ABOUT THE AUTHOR

Andrea Jackson is a graduate of Yale Law School and practiced law for many years before earning her M.F.A. in Creative Writing from the University of Missouri–St. Louis. Her poetry and fiction have been published in many journals, in print and online, and she has been nominated twice for a Pushcart Prize. She is the daughter of Celia Antopolsky and wrote this book in order to better understand her parents' relationship. She lives in St. Louis, Missouri, with her husband of 50 years. They have two adult children and five grandchildren.

CPSIA information can be obtained
at www.ICGtesting.com
Printed in the USA
FFOW03n0202260817
39135FF

9 780692 872383